Teacher Training
On The Go

by Keith D. Johnson

Group
Loveland, Colorado

Group's R.E.A.L. Guarantee® to you:

This Group resource incorporates our R.E.A.L. approach to ministry—one that encourages long-term retention and life transformation. It's ministry that's:

Relational
Because learner-to-learner interaction enhances learning and builds Christian friendships.

Experiential
Because what learners experience through discussion and action sticks with them up to 9 times longer than what they simply hear or read.

Applicable
Because the aim of Christian education is to equip learners to be both hearers and doers of God's Word.

Learner-based
Because learners understand and retain more when the learning process takes into consideration how they learn best.

Visit our Web site: **www.grouppublishing.com**

Credits
Editor: Karl Leuthauser
Chief Creative Officer: Joani Schultz
Copy Editor: Lyndsay E. Gerwing
Art Director: Sharon Anderson
Cover Art Director/Designer: Bambi Eitel
Cover Illustrator: True (Dave Riggins) HGX Design, New York, NY
Illustrator: Joe Stites
Production Manager: Peggy Naylor

Unless otherwise noted, Scripture taken from the HOLY BIBLE, NEW INTERNATIONAL VERSION®. Copyright © 1973, 1978, 1984 by International Bible Society. Used by permission of Zondervan Publishing House. All rights reserved.

ISBN 0-7644-2548-X

10 9 8 7 6 5 4 3 2   12 11 10 09 08 07 06 05 04 03
Printed in the United States of America.

Dedication

I am indebted to so many for their expertise and encouragement in writing this book. For my staff at Group Publishing, including Teresa Strawn, the REAL Learning Specialist manager who nurtures nearly 150 team members throughout the United States; Rebecca Sharp, the Convention and Events manager who ably coordinates all our convention workshops, personnel, and supplies; and Deb Grafel, our tireless administrative assistant in Field Services. I also want to thank Sheila Halasz, one of our ablest, creative, and insightful REAL Specialists, for her contributions to many of the chapters in this book! Thank you, Denise Johnson, my mom, for many of the art suggestions.

I'd like to thank the best leader I have ever worked with, John Geiman, who is a model of "the strenuous life," a seasoned advocate of church growth, and a patient mentor who inspires above-average results.

Thanks to the team at Group Publishing who model growth and effectiveness: Chris Yount for accepting my first article nearly ten years ago and remaining a great friend; Joani Schultz for her passionate and boundless enthusiasm and creative insight; Thom Schultz for his steady courage and measured intellect; Mikal Keefer, whose humor, insight, and feedback I value highly; and my persistently excellent editor, Karl Leuthauser!

Finally, thanks to my wife, Becky, who for nineteen years has believed in me enough to remain my friend, my conscience, and my greatest fan! Thank you, also, Cortney, Cameron, and Christopher for putting up with "Daddy's book" and creating real living examples of faith and growth!

Table of Contents

52 Weeks of Teacher Training on the Go!

Introduction

Time is truly more valuable than money. Is there a single person in your church who has too much time on his or her hands? It seems almost unthinkable to ask your faithful volunteers to carve out more time from their families and responsibilities to attend another teacher-training meeting. However, our responsibility and privilege to effectively teach and encourage children in a safe environment demands skillfully trained teachers.

Maybe you've resorted to bait-and-switch tactics—throw a party and sneak in teacher training at the end. Maybe you've found that the people who attend your meetings are the precious volunteers who need training the least. Maybe you've given up on teacher training altogether.

Teacher Training on the Go provides the training your teachers desperately need without packing even more meetings into your children's ministry calendar. It's difficult to bring teachers to the training sessions, so let's take the training to the teachers! *Teacher Training on the Go* provides 52 photocopiable training sessions that offer help, hope, and practical strategies to *all* of your teachers *every* week. Place copies of the sessions in classrooms, mail them home, or go over them together in a quick pre-teaching devotion and training. Interesting and digestible training sessions feed your teachers a consistent diet of practical insights, inspiration, and proven tricks of the trade.

We know that your training needs are as unique as your ministry. So we've provided some unique delivery mechanisms for the training your teachers so desperately need. You have permission to photocopy each session in this book for use in your church. If you'd rather not spend time at the copy machine, you can also deliver these training sessions *electronically* to your teachers. The CD-ROM attached to the cover of this book provides the same 52 sessions in PDF files for your convenience. Attach each session to an e-mail, and deliver it to your teachers with a few simple clicks. The same CD-ROM also includes 12 "e-couragement" messages as Rich Text Format (RTF) and PDF documents that you can customize, copy, and paste into your e-mail messages to encourage and inspire your teachers. When you need to say thanks or need a new idea to keep your teachers going, use one of the e-couragements to get the word out in a flash. Here's a quick glance at the 12 e-couragements on the CD-ROM:

1. Check Your Attitude
2. Check Your Focus
3. Check Your Preparation
4. Check Your Commitment
5. Check How Interesting You Are
6. Check Your Balance
7. Check Your Patience
8. Check Your Thoughts
9. Check Your Blessings
10. Check Your Example
11. Check Your Resources
12. Check Your Expectations

Some of your teachers may be a little slow in entering the electronic age. Well, don't leave them behind. You'll find an audio CD attached to the cover of this book with 15 audio training sessions. You have our permission to make cassette or CD copies of this CD and hand out the copies to the volunteers at your church. Each session is approximately five minutes long and serves to inspire and train your teachers. Your teachers can listen to the audio training as they drive to church, on the way home, or on the way to work. We know that your teachers are on the go, so we've worked hard to help you send training along with them. Here's a quick glance at the 15 audio training sessions on your CD:

1. Delight Children
2. Surprise Children
3. Arouse Curiosity in Children
4. Encourage Discovery in Children
5. Help Children Learn Through Mistakes
6. Understand Children
7. Teach Children to Crave Wisdom Over Knowledge
8. Be Patient With Children
9. Make Them Comfortable
10. Keep It Interesting
11. Evoke Emotion in Children
12. Encourage Children
13. Enjoy Children
14. Make Them Feel Significant
15. Involve Children

You can pick and choose from these audio training sessions, the 52 photocopiable sessions, and the e-mail e-couragements. Or you can use all three of the tools together to provide weekly training and inspiration to the people who need and deserve it most—your children's ministry volunteers. When volunteers are actively involved in learning, they are enriched. When volunteers interact with other volunteers over topics that improve their success in the classroom *next week*, they are encouraged. When volunteers are consistently shown a better way through meaningful, life-changing training, they are fed. When we feed teachers, we keep them longer, we stretch them wider, and we help them find God's call for their lives. God's blessings as you prepare your teachers to change the world.

I welcome your feedback! If you have any questions or comments, please e-mail me at kjohnson@grouppublishing.com.

The First Day

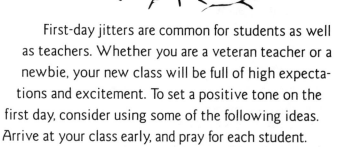

Think It Over

You wake up at 3 a.m. —too early. You wake up at 4 a.m.—still too early. You wake up at 5 a.m.—ugh, still too early. You finally wake up at 6:30 a.m., and you are exhausted! What day is it? It's your first day of class!

the ART of TEACHING

First-day jitters are common for students as well as teachers. Whether you are a veteran teacher or a newbie, your new class will be full of high expectations and excitement. To set a positive tone on the first day, consider using some of the following ideas.

Arrive at your class early, and pray for each student. Make sure the room is set up appropriately for the lesson you'll teach. Put the finishing touches on any decorations you've made. The decorations should communicate "I'm ready for you" and "I'm glad you're here" to the children and their parents as they arrive. It's important that you work to make children feel comfortable and to help them have fun. When children arrive, greet them at their level and acknowledge their parents. You might want to go over expectations during class, but don't spend your whole time on the rules.

Try to encourage getting acquainted rather than focus on intense learning. The first day sets the tone, but it should be more relational than informational. Let your students get to know *you*. A great game to play is to list on a sheet of paper four facts about you. Three of the facts should be true, and one should be false. Have the students try to guess which ones are true and which is false.

Let your students get to know *each other*. A fun game to play with older children is to have children arrange themselves in alphabetical order by last name and then have each child share one thing about himself or herself that starts with the first letter of his or her last name. For example, Madeline Lang might say, "I'm Madeline Lang, and I love licorice." Whatever activities you use, make sure you help children understand that your class is the place they *want* to be every Sunday.■

Take It Home

On index cards, write the name of each child who will be in your class or small group. List children's phone numbers, birth dates, and parents names. Finally, try to get some personal information about them that will help you pray for them, learn about them, and understand the goals that their families have for their learning. Then follow up by praying for them regularly.

Check It Out

Pilots of airplanes have checklists they review before each takeoff. Captains of ships have detailed checklists they go over with their crew prior to weighing anchor and departing from port. A checklist is a great tool to help novices or pros make sure they are prepared before they start anything!

One boat owner failed to even type up a checklist, let alone review one. Upon pulling his new boat out of the lake after the first "shakedown" trip, he failed to secure *both* tie-down lines. As the boat was pulled up the ramp, the boat rolled off the trailer and onto the concrete surface of the road!

Have you checked your checklist?

It's time for a CHANGE

Lord, help me continue to be prepared for my class and to prepare for the future by...

SCRIPTURES to Study
*Commit it to MEMORY

"But seek first his kingdom and his righteousness, and all these things will be given to you as well."

—Matthew 6:33

■ What should your priorities be as you begin your teaching year?

■ What kind of things does God add to teachers who first seek God's kingdom?

Who Said THAT?

"Most adults will do anything to avoid going to a party where they don't know anyone. But for some reason, we may be impatient with the young child who hesitates on the first day of school...where there are no familiar faces."

—Cathy Ridner Tempelsman

The Eyes of a Child

Think It Over

Children are not little adults, yet we somehow arrange our classrooms to reflect *our* adult preferences. Picture your classroom right now. Does it focus on children and their needs? Does it focus on teachers and their needs?

When I was your age, I had to walk to school with snow up to my thighs!

the ART of TEACHING

You know the phrase "It's like riding a bike." For most adults, riding a bike is not a problem. For a child who has just taken off the training wheels, riding a bike is terrifying!

What was riding a bike like when you did it for the first time? Do you remember how much you wanted to ride? But by the time you sat on the bicycle, desire gave way to fear! Chances are an adult in your life tried to accommodate your age, size, and ability to improve your chances of success.

An adult put you on a small bike so that if you fell, you wouldn't fall far; held you long enough for you to catch your balance; stood behind you so you could see where you were going. An adult picked you up after you fell, and an adult encouraged you to try again!

Your success was due, in large part, to a big person's persistence and patience to adapt his or her training to your capacity to learn. The opposite, unfortunately, is also true. An impatient, do-what-I-say, or demanding authoritarian who insists on an adult bike might produce results. However, rather than fostering joy in riding, the overbearing instructor creates bad memories and a lifelong avoidance of bicycle riding.

We are often blinded in our own efforts to teach because we see through adult eyes and adult experiences. We sometimes try to impose our own childhood experiences on the children in our classroom. Identifying with children helps us to communicate with them. When you come to teach a passage of Scripture, you often are retelling a story that is so familiar to you that it's like riding a bike. You could probably teach it without even looking up the passage in the Bible. But what is it like for a child hearing it for the first time?

We can only be heard and our learners will only understand if the level of instruction fits with their capacity. To be child-centered is as simple as speaking to a child at his or her eye level, talking in a voice that is calm and reassuring, creating space that encourages discovery and choices, or simply putting graphics and pictures at a child's eye level. What are some other ways to make your classroom child-centered? ∎

Keep Up

Growing up in a house full of four brothers and sisters, we were always in competition with one another. One day, before my mother came home from work, we decided to have a contest to see which one of us was the best artist. We drew our pictures, and I was sure that when mom came home, she would choose my drawing. My mother, a single parent, took our bait. She took all five of the drawings and went into the next room to "grade" them. Seated on a couch, we couldn't wait for her verdict. "Today we will award the prizes for the best drawings," my mother began. "In the three-year-old division, Priscilla receives an A+. In the five-year-old division..."

Sometimes it is difficult for us to be child-centered because we forget what it was like to learn something new or see something for the first time. Try driving to work using a different route from that which you normally drive. What did you like about this new route? What didn't you like?

Shop at a new grocery store each time you need food this week. What did it feel like when you were looking for products you needed? Did you ask for help or try to figure it out on your own?

SCRIPTURES to Study
Commit it to MEMORY

"And he said: 'I tell you the truth, unless you change and become like little children, you will never enter the kingdom of heaven.' "

—Matthew 18:3

■ In what way do you need to become more like a little child?

■ How do you need to change you classroom environment or teaching style to be more child-friendly?

It's time for a CHANGE

God is showing me that I need to stop being childish when I...

God, please help me to be more childlike as I...

"All grown-ups were once children—although few of them remember it."

—Antoine de Saint Exupéry,
The Little Prince

Problems With Behavior Problems

"When Amaziah returned from slaughtering the Edomites, he brought back the gods of Seir."

Think It Over

the ART of TEACHING

How do you feel after teaching a class in which things are completely out of control? How do the children feel? What happened that led to the last time your class was out of control? What could you have done differently?

There are some very obvious expectations you have for the children in your class. Your children probably know that they must arrive on time, come prepared to learn, dress according to normal standards, behave appropriately, and exit when the big people who brought them arrive.

There are clear expectations of what you are to do in your class too. You prepare for your lesson, arrive prior to the children to set up, and deliver the lesson as you keep children safe.

Simple! If it weren't for the distractions of behavior problems, you and your children would have a blast! But that is not always the case. Temper tantrums happen, emotions explode, fidgeting overwhelms, or talking interrupts. Behavior problems are bound to occur, but they don't have to sink your lesson. You can take some simple steps to stop behavior problems before they start.

Begin by really getting to know your children. Many public and private schools send out a questionnaire to each parent prior to the start of the school year. This helps teachers get acquainted with the children they'll greet the first day of school. They often have great open-ended questions, such as "What special personality strength can I encourage in your child this year?"

If one of your children has difficulty in your class, involve his or her parents to get tips on the best methods of intervention and prevention. As you get to know your children, you'll learn to prevent negative reactions to transitions, downtime, and other events that spark behavior problems. Prevention is your most powerful weapon in behavior modification.

The most essential aspect of prevention is preparation. As you prepare, listen to what God has to say to *you* through the lesson. Your preparation should include understanding age-level characteristics and thinking on how your staff or other volunteers can use their strengths in the classroom so you don't feel alone. Make certain you are ready for the lesson with all supplemental materials in place and unnecessary distractions removed. Your preparation should include arriving early enough to nonverbally tell that first child, "I'm ready for you!" Your attitude, confidence, and effectiveness are often proportionate to your preparation.

Despite your best preparation, behavior problems are bound to occur. When they do, try to interrupt your lesson as little as possible. For example, if a child is whispering while you are talking, start by giving the child a knowing glance. If that doesn't work, gently place your hand on the child's shoulder while you continue talking. If the child continues to talk, ask him or her to refrain from talking until you've finished. Talk with other teachers to determine what methods of intervention they've found to be most effective for the most challenging children.

Your classroom doesn't have to be stuffy or boring. In fact, controlled chaos is sometimes the best learning environment. However, rude interruptions and disrespectful actions ruin the lesson for everyone. Be ready to head off these behaviors before they become problems for you and your classroom. ■

Modified Behavior

The two boys were known around the church as troublemakers. They routinely tested the patience of Sunday school teachers, superintendents, and even the pastor during his sermon. Not wanting these fatherless boys to create havoc during his charge—and seeing their mother in the choir—the head usher hit on a plan.

Pulling Daniel and his brother aside before one service, Mr. Gunnels asked them for a favor. He asked these two to go up in the balcony during the sermon and count each side of the sanctuary. One would take one side and another the other side. Sensing the importance of the job and hearing the word *balcony*, which had for so long been off limits, the two boys jumped at the opportunity.

They often made a competition out of the job, hoping to have more people on one side than the other. Sunday after Sunday, the two boys waited patiently for the cue of the pastor to begin his sermon before they embarked on the head usher's creative plan. In time, counting was given to someone else, but the boys kept focus in church and even listened during the sermon!

SCRIPTURES to Study
Commit it to MEMORY

"But the fruit of the Spirit is love, joy, peace, patience, kindness, goodness, faithfulness, gentleness and self-control. Against such things there is no law."

—Galatians 5:22-23

■ Which fruit of the Spirit is first seen by those around you when you are faced with a problem?

■ Which fruit of the Spirit is most absent in you when things go wrong in the classroom?

Take It Home

Sometimes the way we request compliance or set up an activity promotes behavior mishaps. Try this with a group of preschoolers or young children. Ask them to get into a circle without giving any other directions. What do you see happening? Why do you think they are having problems getting into a circle? What are some creative ways to get children into a circle? How can you help children to do the following tasks in creative ways?

■ **Pick up their toys.**

■ **Get ready for prayer.**

■ **Participate in singing.**

TIC... TOC... TIC...

It's time for a CHANGE

God, help me prepare better for my students by...

Who Said THAT?

"Problems cannot be solved by the same level of thinking that created them."

—Albert Einstein

Discipline That Disciples

Think It Over

The words *discipline* and *disciple* are both derived from the same Latin word, *discipulus.* What do the two words have in common? Why do we most often associate *discipline* with pain and frustration rather than the positive results of being a fully devoted disciple?

the ART of TEACHING

The illustration above contains a car that is clearly out of gas. In order to function properly, the car must get fuel. To get fuel, the car must either be pushed or simply steered—it all depends on the slope of the ground. The same illustration parallels our own efforts to discipline children. We can push children against their will in a constant struggle, or we can gently steer them in a direction that helps them function properly.

We steer children when we tap into what truly motivates them. If a child in your class needs to express himself verbally, provide opportunities for appropriate talking and discussion. If a child needs to fidget, provide opportunities in your lesson to move around. If you have children who are moving or talking at an inappropriate time, remind them that their time is coming to talk and to move around. Encourage them that you'll soon give them a chance to do what they need to do if they can just hang on.

Remember that the goal of your discipline is to make disciples. If children are put in timeout because they lie or fight, let them know that they will be able to rejoin the class when they apologize or tell the truth. Timeout is not the goal. Shame is not the goal. The goal is to help children make the right choice in the future and to make the right choice in the present. The amount of time spent in timeout should be dependent upon when the child is again ready to learn.

We push children when we reward with a bribe, when we punish, or even when we repeatedly remind them of our expectations to the point of nagging. This motivation is external to them and, therefore, not "owned" by them. My mother taught me a simple discipline technique that may be helpful. When you take away something with which a child is playing that might be dangerous or toxic, immediately replace it with something with which the child *can* play. In your classroom, if a child is paging through a book but not working on a craft as you explain the craft project, gently remove the book and replace it with the craft items. You want to help the misbehaving child change direction. As a teacher, you have a choice in making it difficult or easy on you and the child. ■

Learning by Doing

Dr. Maria Montessori began by simply observing. As children came into her classroom, she was surprised to discover that children would gravitate toward the teaching supplies she offered instead of to the toys. By adapting her methods and offering activities such as gymnastics and gardening, she fueled the children's innate desire for learning. If a child misbehaved, he or she was simply given nothing to do.

"The children soon started asking Montessori to teach them to read and write. So she devised sandpaper letters that they could touch and trace, pronouncing the sounds as they did so. One day during recess, a 5-year-old boy cried excitedly, 'I can write!' and wrote the word *mano*—hand—

with chalk on the pavement. Other children began writing, too, and news of the miraculous 4- and 5-year-olds who taught themselves to write traveled quickly."

—From "Madam Montessori" by Nancy Shute, Smithsonian Magazine (September 2002)

SCRIPTURES to Study
Commit it to MEMORY

"All Scripture is God-breathed and is useful for teaching, rebuking, correcting and training in righteousness, so that the man of God may be thoroughly equipped for every good work."

—2 Timothy 3:16-17

■ How do teaching, rebuking, correcting, and training work together?

■ How are they different?

Take It Home

Jesus often used the tasks and leisure activities in which his disciples engaged to train them. For example, he used fishing, sailing, eating, sleeping, and household chores to teach about the kingdom of God. Spend a day this week either watching your own children or observing children at a McDonald's PlayPlace, and write down everything you see them do. Compare your list with what you've planned in your classroom. How is your plan similar or dissimilar to what children naturally like to do? What is one thing you can take from this experience and implement next week in your classroom?

It's time for a CHANGE

I have trouble with a child in my class. I really don't know the way he or she should go. I think you are directing me to...

Who Said THAT?

"The idle brain is the devil's playground."

—"Professor Harold Hill," Meredith Wilson's *The Music Man*

Plan Something for Them, or They'll Plan Something for You

The sermon was so fantastic that I guess the pastor just lost track of time.

Think It Over

The lesson couldn't have gone better if Moses himself had given it. The only hitch? You finished about fifteen minutes before the parents were to arrive! What do you do next?

the ART of TEACHING

When I was a child, our elementary Sunday school teacher led us in a lot of "Sword Drills." Maybe you experienced something similar. We would all hold our Bibles in our laps, and the teacher would say something like "Micah...chapter 7...verse 4." Then after a pause she would say, "Go!" Twenty eager kids, motivated by a piece of hard candy, quickly turned the pages until one deft-of-hand child stood and began reading, "The best of them is like a brier, the most upright worse than a thorn hedge. The day of your watchmen has come, the day God visits you. Now is the time of their confusion."

I only found out later that these fun, though disconnected, activities were simply time-fillers. They were additions in the Sunday school hour due to long worship services or special speakers. What do you do when your best-laid plans don't work out, come up short, or take a direction you did not plan? Don't panic! Try these lesson stretchers:

■ Prepare a few extra activities that will enhance your lesson. If you prepare in advance, you won't just fill time; you'll use it. Activities that require no or few supplies are easiest to implement. Game books such as *The Humongous Book of Games for Children's Ministry* (Group Publishing) provide great game ideas for almost every major Bible story.

■ Bring the songs you've sung to life by adding motions. Having children create their own motions will help them learn the meaning of the words they sing.

■ Take Scripture memory verses deeper by having children create murals based on the Scriptures on your windows using dry-erase markers. Make sure you test the markers so you know that they'll wipe off.

■ Review your Bible stories with actions and movement in a call-respond method in which the kids imitate rain (rubbing hands together, snapping fingers, patting legs, stomping feet), create lightning (blinking or turning off lights), and make other background effects.

■ Foster deeper discussion with more questions answered in groups of two or three rather than all together!

Finally, never let 'em see you sweat. Unlike school during the week, you don't have a bell, a lunch, or a bus schedule to keep. This is not clockwork; this is church, and we are a family that sometimes likes to talk. Relax! Enjoy the extra time you have to connect, build relationships, and encourage Christian friendships. ■

Now let's include a ring for all of our second cousins' pets.

Creative Delight

During my work with the Billy Graham Evangelistic Association, we had many discussions on how to keep the attention of a stadium full of kids prior to the start of the program. We needed time-fillers! We came up with some ingenious (and not so ingenious) ideas—from roving clowns on stilts in the stands to huge beach balls that were batted around (some popping with a loud bang). But the two ideas that worked the best were arrived at by sheer accident.

In 1998, the winter after hurricane Mitch, Managua, Nicaragua, had its share of poverty. Unemployment was nearly 70 percent, and with nearly 160,000 children expected at our rallies in Managua, entrepreneurs of all ages naturally worked to cash in. The amount of food for sale in the stadium, whether cooked in the aisles, cooked in the baseball field on makeshift drums, or just wheeled on carts, made the organizers unhappy but sure made the crowds smile.

In 1999 in Kiev, Ukraine, our cameras were warming up as the kids were arriving, and kids were pointing as they saw their pictures on the large image magnification televisions at the front of the Sports Palace. We used the tools we had to delight and entertain the children as they arrived!

Take It Home

One reason children tend to misbehave during a long car trip is that they have nothing to do. Talk to at least four adults with young children and ask them what they have done to make a long drive go quickly. If you have children and are planning a road trip, take some time during the next mealtime together to ask for suggestions of activities to do during the travel on your next trip.

It's time for a CHANGE

Lord, help me to trust in you when...

SCRIPTURES to Study
* Commit it to MEMORY

"Trust in the Lord with all your heart and lean not on your own understanding; in all your ways acknowledge him, and he will make your paths straight."

—Proverbs 3:5-6

■ What does this verse say about planning for the unexpected?

■ How can you "acknowledge him" in all your teaching ways?

Who Said THAT?

"No one is so brave that he is not disturbed by something unexpected."

—Julius Caesar

Feeding the Cook: Nurturing Your Own Growth

Here, let me help you up!

Who is holding you up?

Think It Over

A branch that is cut from a vine appears healthy for a day or two after it has been cut. However, the branch really starts dying the second it is cut off. You may appear healthy and fruitful to your students. However, are you connected to the Vine? If you are not connected with Christ, you are dying. Eventually, your condition will be apparent, and your fruit will wither.

the ART of TEACHING

The Greeks loved their actors. The Greek word for *actor* was *hypokrités. Hypokrités* is the direct ancestor of the English word *hypocrite.* Today a hypocrite is an actor of the worst sort. Hypocrisy in spiritual leaders is the most dangerous form of acting, as spiritual leaders are guiding (or misleading) people in eternal matters.

Every leader has periods of spiritual strength as well as weakness. Spiritual struggles are not necessarily an indication that a person should stop leading or teaching. However, a teacher must stay connected with Jesus if he or she is to continue leading, teaching, and ministering to others.

Here are some easy opportunities for teachers to get fed and avoid becoming hypocrites, playing roles in front of kids.

■ Attend church, classes, and meetings to connect with other Christians. Your pursuit of growth and relationship with God will impact children as they witness your example. Children will also benefit from the light, passion, and life that your growth brings to the class.

■ *Really* show up when you attend worship. Listen attentively to the sermon. Worship God with your heart and not just your voice. Be eager to understand what God is saying to you today.

■ Look for opportunities to give of your time, talents, and treasures. Quietly but sincerely share your resources so that God's work can increase. Amazingly, giving away often fills us up. For example, you could go without a meal once a week as you hand-feed one of the shut-ins your church has taken under its wings.

■ Pray with your spouse, children, or friends at the end of the day to conclude a day of stress on a sweet note. Pray quietly when your heart is heavy. Pray with gusto when you're ready to rejoice. Pray for your students by name throughout the week.

■ Find times for rest. Even Jesus went away to be with his Father during hectic times in his ministry. Remember Mary and Martha? Martha worked at a hectic pace. Mary sat at Jesus' feet. When Martha complained, Jesus said, "Only one thing is needed. Mary has chosen what is better" (Luke 10:42).

There's no time for acting when we are clinging to Jesus, the Vine. Isn't it interesting that John states that when we bear fruit, God prunes it—literally cuts it off—so that we can bear more fruit? So remember that fruit you thought you had a few months ago? It has been harvested. Time to bear more fruit! ■

Save Yourself

Those who live in cold climates are aware of the dangers of thin ice. If someone falls through thin ice, hypothermia and death are imminent. A person who has hypothermia will flounder, soon surrender, and drown. According to *The Merck Manual of Medical Information*, "the onset of hypothermia is usually so gradual and subtle that neither the victim nor others realize what's happening.  Movement becomes slow and clumsy, reaction time is longer, the mind is blurred, judgment is impaired, and hallucinations occur." You may think you are helping the victim when you jump in to rescue him or her. But you could become a casualty of the cold and need help yourself!

It's interesting that flight attendants state, "In the event of a loss of cabin pressure, oxygen masks will appear overhead. Place the mask on your face first by securely pulling on the straps. If travelling with young children, place the mask on your face first and then secure your child's mask."

Your ability to help someone else is affected by your own health and safety.

 **Take It Home**

Watch one sports event this week that you haven't really watched in the past and in which you have never actually participated. It could be a NASCAR race, a professional football game, or even a round of golf. Try to watch for at least fifteen minutes.

Answer the following questions:

■ How long did it take you to figure out what was going on?

■ How would your understanding of the sport be different if you had participated in it?

■ Why is it important to participate in your own relationship with God if you are teaching children about God?

SCRIPTURES to Study
* Commit it to MEMORY

"I am the vine; you are the branches. If a man remains in me and I in him, he will bear much fruit; apart from me you can do nothing."

—John 15:5

■ How is your teaching affected by your connection to Christ?

■ How do you stay connected to Christ?

TIC... TOC... TIC...

It's time for a CHANGE

God, I feel connected to you when I...

 **Who Said THAT?**

"If you stop growing today, you stop teaching tomorrow."

—Howard Hendricks,
Teaching to Change Lives

Team Ministry

That's my husband. I think he is just a taller kid.

Think It Over

Why is it that some teaching teams just seem to be so close, collegial, and have so much fun together? How could your team work together better?

the ART of TEACHING

Do you communicate well with your co-workers or classroom helpers? Or do you dread seeing them at church—feeling a bit of relief if you don't see them on Sunday? The best advertisement your children's ministry can create to either repel or compel volunteers is the health of your team's relationship!

Your success in working together with others is dependent on your ability to communicate with them. You may not have a choice about the people with whom you work, so you must work to understand their unique qualities and quirks. It is interesting that people often lose their jobs or leave their jobs because they do not get along with their co-workers.

Viktor Frankl, Auschwitz survivor and the author of *Man's Search for Meaning* writes, "We who lived in concentration camps can remember the men who walked through the huts comforting others, giving away their last piece of bread. They may have been few in number, but they offer sufficient proof that everything can be taken from a man but one thing: the last of the human freedoms—to choose one's attitude in any given set of circumstances, to choose one's own way." The attitude you choose toward others will have a tremendous impact on your ability to work well with them.

Remember that conflict can be a source of growth rather than a point of despair! Not only is conflict inevitable, but it is often corporately and personally beneficial. What pianist hasn't had to endure hardship to play brilliantly, or what sports team has not endured a little pain to achieve great gain? Don't look for conflict, but when it comes, don't avoid it. Relax and remember that conflict is an essential part of relationship. ■

Do you think our team may be a little too well-oiled?

Whose Way?

"A few years ago two ministers got into a fight about what they considered to be an important doctrinal matter. They settled the fight when the first minister told the second: 'Look, what are we fighting over? We're both striving to do the Lord's work. You do it your way and I'll do it His way!'"

—*Illustrations Unlimited*

SCRIPTURES *to Study*
✱ Commit it to MEMORY

"As a prisoner for the Lord, then, I urge you to live a life worthy of the calling you have received. Be completely humble and gentle; be patient, bearing with one another in love. Make every effort to keep the unity of the Spirit through the bond of peace."

—Ephesians 4:1-3

■ How can you keep the "unity of the Spirit" in your team today?

■ How have you been "bearing with" your co-workers at church?

Take It Home

Try this experiment one morning this week. Ask your spouse or child to help you make eggs and bacon. Put the eggs and bacon in two separate pans on the stove. Tie your ankles together with a rope, and put your arms around each other. Leave your right hand free and your partner's left hand free, and try to make the bacon and eggs. When you have finished giggling and are hopefully not burned or hurt, sit down to eat and answer the following questions:

■ What was the most difficult part of working together when you had to?

■ How is that like or unlike trying to work with others to accomplish something important?

It's time for a CHANGE

TIC... TOC... TIC...

Lord, help me humble myself this week by...

Who Said THAT?

"Grief can take care of itself, but to get the full value of a joy you must have somebody to divide it with."

—Mark Twain,
*Following the Equator:
A Journey Around the World*

Tell Me a Story

Can we hear that story again?

Think It Over

Teaching isn't telling, and learning isn't listening! Telling a story is captivating only if your students are carried *into* the story and the story is carried *out* of the classroom.

That's the same story we heard two years ago.

the ART of TEACHING

Storytelling is fundamentally about communication. You have communicated when there is a connection between the Bible and the life of your listener.

One excellent communicator of the twentieth century was Ronald Reagan. The coach who helped Ronald Reagan succeed was Roger Ailes, the current president of Fox News. He wrote a little book a few years ago called *You Are the Message*. In the book, he summarized four essentials of a great communicator:

- Be prepared.
- Make others comfortable.
- Be committed.
- Be interesting.

Simple, isn't it? The worst way to tell a story is the way you *always* tell a story. When you *prepare* your story to make your class *comfortable*, demonstrate *commitment* about your topic and to your audience, and are *interesting*, the story will come alive. You don't have to be the world's best storyteller for children. They'll find you interesting if you simply show confidence and provide opportunities for them to get involved.

You can build confidence and find creative opportunities for involvement by spending time in preparation. Spend time with the story, thinking about what images and thoughts will come to a child as you read. Work on painting a picture for their imaginations by including props, making comparisons to modern equivalents, and expressing the likely feelings and thought processes of the characters. You can increase variety by using simple sound effects for water, wind, or birds. You can use movement, classroom interaction, or video clips, or invite guests to tell stories or even act them out.

If you're new to storytelling, don't be afraid of overacting. You most likely need to become more expressive in your reading. Use gestures and expressions to convey wonder, sorrow, and even anger. As you share the story, concentrate on going slowly. Children need time to absorb your words and to picture the details. Bring children into the story by asking questions about the emotions, pictures, and details.

Be flexible as you tell stories. If you are interrupted during the story, don't let it shake you. You can even think quickly about ways to include the interruption into the story. If you are at ease and having fun, children will follow right along with you. A well-told story will leave children wanting more! ■

I'm glad our teacher brought her Bible today.

A Seasoned Storyteller —

Author and Sunday school teacher John Grisham told a group of students at Baylor University how his Christian faith influences his writing. While waiting for *A Time to Kill* to get published, he began working on a second novel, *The Firm*. His agent encouraged him to spice it up with more sex and violence, but he refused.

Grisham told the audience how he came home to the sound of the telephone ringing. His agent told him the movie rights had been sold for $600,000. His life changed from that moment on, but not his faith.

Take It Home

Open your Sunday school lesson to the main story or section that contains the Bible story. Note how it is written. Oftentimes, publishers will have you read the story with a call-and-response method. Sometimes the children will be asked to act out the story. During the week look for other ways people tell stories. For example, you could watch how the news, a movie, a newspaper article, or even a co-worker tells a story. Look for ways to incorporate those methods into your storytelling.

It's time for a **CHANGE**

Lord, help me give meaning to your world by...

SCRIPTURES to Study
✱ Commit it to MEMORY

"They read from the Book of the Law of God, making it clear and giving the meaning so that the people could understand what was being read."

—Nehemiah 8:8

■ How can you know if your class has understood what the Bible says?

■ What should you say to your class if you don't understand?

Who Said **THAT?**

"I like a good story well told. That is the reason I am sometimes forced to tell them myself."

—Mark Twain,
"The Watermelon" speech

Taking Off Without Leaving

Helen has been teaching for 30 years and has never asked for a single day off.

Think It Over

Service requires a measure of self-sacrifice. But servants who resent serving, feel burned out, or are just plain bored are most likely doing more harm than good through their service. What will it take for you to serve with a renewed attitude and a right heart?

the ART of TEACHING

You feel the tug to quit, but you only want to take a break! Quitting would make your pain go away. It would also create distance with the leader who recruited you. Worst of all, quitting would short-change the investment you've made in the students and cause you to miss out on the opportunity to see the fruit of your good work! Here are a few secrets that will help you keep serving.

Remember that you are part of a team that needs you. You would never just forget to show up or just show up late because you had a tough time getting going. You are a faithful and important part of the team. Since you matter, talk to your leader about your feelings, and look to your team for support. You'll find that they probably have the same thoughts every now and then!

Make sure your efforts are focused in the right places. Many businesses work to make sure they don't build qualities that customers don't care about in their products. For example, customers aren't looking for blenders that have built-in radios—they want blenders that mix well and that continue to work. Do your children really need you to study the original Greek and Hebrew so they can effectively grasp the point of the Bible passage? What is your goal in teaching? What are you doing that doesn't achieve that goal? Remember why you signed up in the first place, and hold onto the experiences that have helped you make it this far.

It may be helpful to evaluate your expectations. Is it realistic to expect that a large group of eight-year-olds will sit quietly in your class for an hour without getting fidgety? Modify your goals and expectations to the real needs and personalities in your class. Rather than setting out to help children grasp the concept of sanctification, you might want them to simply understand that God helps them grow. Continue to challenge children, but realistically assess what you can accomplish in your class.

Don't be afraid to ask your leader for a break. Leaders want volunteers who are thriving and enjoying themselves. It is much more manageable to cover a break than to replace a position. Rather than taking a long sabbatical, consider scheduling in routine breaks that keep refreshing you. For example, rather than taking the quarter off, consider taking off one week every month for a time. Remember that your first priority should be to your family and then to your adopted family—the children whose spiritual lives you are nurturing each Sunday. ■

Take It Home

Do you have a substitute list? Call a school principal or teacher, and ask him or her two questions: "What is your procedure for finding a substitute?" and "What has surprised you the most about your pool of substitutes?" Talk with your children's ministry leader or other teachers about creating a substitute list.

It's time for a CHANGE

Lord, give me the strength to continue when I feel...

Fan the Flame

Forest fires burn out when a firefighter eliminates one of the three necessary ingredients: oxygen, fuel, or heat. What is causing your fire to go out? In your fire for serving, think of the oxygen as the thing you cannot see: God's Spirit. Think of the fuel as the Word of God and the heat as your own emotional and physical energy. Don't let your fire go out!

SCRIPTURES to Study
Commit it to MEMORY

"Restore to me the joy of your salvation."

—Psalm 51:12a

■ How can you lose your joy in teaching?

■ According to this verse, who is the one who restores your joy?

Who Said THAT?

"It's not work, if you love what you're doing."

—Steve Sears

Moving From Knowledge to Wisdom

I want them to know they're growing.

Think It Over

In schools, children are given grades to determine their levels of proficiency. Grades seem too subjective and judgmental when it comes to measuring spiritual growth. How can Sunday school teachers effectively assess if children are growing spiritually?

the ART of TEACHING

It has been called the most important hour of the week! It is hard to disagree with Sunday school's importance, but measuring results is often difficult. There is, however, a key ingredient to effectiveness that every teacher should know: The difference between knowledge and wisdom.

Knowledge is the foundation for confidence in living the Christian life. We either know what God expects or we do not. Knowledge comes through reading, listening, experiencing, and practice. We tell stories that we hope children will hear and understand. We ask questions that assist children to confirm whether or not they understand what we've taught. Your "hand-raisers" make it appear that you're getting somewhere as they quickly throw up their hands to give answers for every question. But knowledge is not the highest goal of our teaching. Scripture indicates a higher goal that should be the final measure for any effective teacher.

Wisdom is the correct application of the knowledge we possess. It is the great equalizer in the classroom because it asks not "What do you know?" but "What did you *do* with what you know?" The late theologian and thinker Francis Schaeffer did not ask, "What should we then know?" as if knowledge were the key to the Christian's success. Instead, in his book and subsequent film series, he asked, "*How Should We Then Live?*" James, the brother of Jesus, writes, "be ye *doers* of the word, and not hearers only" (James 1:22, King James Version).

Jesus reminded his disciples that they were to "teach them to *observe*"; that is, teach the people they want to reach to *do* not just *know.* If anyone lacks wisdom, Scripture states, they should ask God and he'll give "liberally" and not withhold it! Unlike knowledge, which depends on mental clarity and "smarts," wisdom is something we *all* can possess! ■

I'm Sorry!

A Wise Response

During one of the training sessions for the 1996 Twin Cities Billy Graham Crusade, I made a careless slip of the tongue that threatened to alienate one whole denomination. I received a call from Al Quie, chairman of our event and the former governor of Minnesota, requesting me to come to his office. I was truly honored and excited to speak privately with a man who was so instrumental in Chuck Colson's decision to become a Christian. "And now," I thought, "he wants to meet with me!"

Speaking in deliberate cadences the governor began, "Keith, many times in my career, I've said some things I've regretted." A knot began to form in my own stomach as I began to realize just how different this meeting was turning out to be. "The best course of action is to step up and apologize to all parties that you offended."

"You're right, sir" was all I could squeak out as I signed the pre-printed letter of apology that was sitting on his desk.

SCRIPTURES to Study
Commit it to MEMORY

"The fear of the Lord is the beginning of knowledge, but fools despise wisdom and discipline."

—Proverbs 1:7

■ What is the fear of the Lord?

■ How are discipline and wisdom connected?

Take It Home

Testing for knowledge is fairly straightforward. Multiple choice, fill in the blank, and true/false questions are some of the more popular methods used to assess knowledge. Wisdom, however, is the application of the knowledge you have. This week, try to match what you *know* with what you *do* to see how you rate personally. Think about how you applied your knowledge in the following areas:

■ Did you keep your commitments this week? Were you on time?

■ Did you stay within your budget?

■ Did you reach out to and love your family and friends? your extended family?

■ Did you spend time in Scripture? Did you spend time in prayer?

It's time for a CHANGE

Lord, shape my will and desire to obey you by...

Who Said THAT?

"Wisdom is knowing what to do next; virtue is doing it."

—David Starr Jordan,
The Philosophy of Hope

Helping Children Love God

*I can't depend on my legs
to carry me anymore...
I can't depend on this chair sometimes,
but I can depend on God all the time!
I want you to learn to trust him
in your life too!*

Think It Over

Think about all the things you love without any particular order of importance. We love kittens or puppies, sunshine, tulips, back rubs, shopping at our stores, music, and money in birthday cards. It's easy to love something we experience but much harder to love what we don't know!

the ART of TEACHING

Arranged marriages are still practiced by many different cultures. One family decides its child should marry the child from another family at a predetermined date. The choice is made regardless of how the two *feel* about each other. What about love? It will come in time—and if it doesn't, it's really not that important.

To force children to love God without understanding is like an arranged marriage. We are placing the action and knowledge of loving God over and above their feelings for God. But just as it is inherently wrong to place feelings above our actions, so its opposite is also full of problems.

Scripture tells us to love the Lord our God with all our heart, soul, and strength. In the balance of our heart, soul, and strength, we can fully connect with God. How is that done? Humans connect in courtship, conversation, and sharing experiences. Similarly, we need to show children how to spend time with God, pray to God, and share experiences with God. Children need to know what God has done and what God is like in order for them to form a passion for or even an opinion about God.

Tell children the stories of what God has done! What better way to get to know what God is like than to see what God has accomplished. Stories in Scripture tell of God's faithfulness, God's love, and God's character more than a sterile list or memorized creed. Work to link the stories of the Bible to personal examples. Your own experience with God and your student's stories create a wonderful correlation between the world of history told in the Bible and a child's life today.

Love is always associated with action in Scripture. Love does stuff! Jesus asked Peter if he loved him. Peter said, "Yes, you know I do." Jesus then responded, "Feed my sheep." In other words, "Then do something!" Love and obedience go hand in hand. If we love God, we do what he wants. Your classroom should reflect this observation by making practical applications of every story, every lesson, and every question. ∎

A Lot of Love

Valentine's Day candy sales were projected to top $1.05 billion in 2003, and 110 million roses were expected to be sent, according to the National Retail Federation. The poll of 1,000 respondents also found that 80.0 percent of Valentines planned to give greeting cards, 58.7 percent anticipated taking their sweetheart out for the evening, 36.9 percent were going to give flowers, and 30.9 percent planned to give candy.

But love seems to be a last-minute thought for most people. According to ACNielsen, "Valentine's day week generates more candy sales than any other holiday week." According to Phil Lempert, food trends editor for NBC's *Today Show*, "It appears that people tend to plan ahead when buying candy for Christmas, Halloween, and Easter, whereas Valentine's Day generates more last-minute candy buying."

SCRIPTURES to Study
*Commit it to MEMORY

"We love because he first loved us."

—1 John 4:19

■ When was the first time you felt that God loved you?

■ How do you live out your love for God?

Take It Home

This week pick out a special relationship that you have, and make a point of doing something about it.

■ **MONDAY:** Send a card telling the person what you appreciate about him or her and why.

■ **TUESDAY:** Cook the person's favorite meal.

■ **WEDNESDAY:** Watch the person's favorite show.

■ **THURSDAY:** Clean up after someone you love without letting him or her know what you did.

■ **FRIDAY:** Fix something that is broken for someone you love.

■ **SATURDAY:** Spend time with someone you love doing what *he or she* would normally do on that day.

TIC... TOC... TIC...

It's time for a CHANGE

Help me love you more, Lord, by...

Who Said THAT?

"A career is wonderful, but you can't curl up with it on a cold night."

—Marilyn Monroe

Attendance Boosters

I couldn't be that late!

Think It Over

How do you feel
when a student
doesn't show up for
that lesson you just
knew he or she would
love? How can you
turn your disappoint-
ment and discourage-
ment into action by
creating a class that
students will feel
sorry to miss?

the ART of TEACHING

You can't increase student achievement without increasing student participation! You can't have any of your students participating if they don't show up. What can a Sunday school teacher do to enhance the attendance of those students who, while on the class roster, rarely or inconsistently attend? Even though children aren't completely in control of their Sunday school attendance, you can have an impact on turnout.

It's important to recognize that your students are children. Children don't drive to church. They might only spend every other weekend with their churchgoing parent, or their parents may be sporadic attendees. Attendance charts actually punish kids by noting who is *not* in attendance. Never point out how many times a child has missed your class. Rather, celebrate each child's attendance and participation. Warmly welcome infrequent attendees' arrival by telling them how glad you are that they are there.

When children don't attend, let them know what they've missed and that they are missed. Send a card, make a phone call, or just send home the lesson they missed with a note. Emphasize that you hope to see them next Sunday without focusing on the past.

Work to make every class the best it can be. Make your opening the best part of the day! Start on time, and remember that the minute the first student arrives is the moment class begins. If you delay or continually restart the class, you're rewarding the last person. Don't start with a large-group activity. It is difficult to be late and arrive to a large group in which you cannot find your friends. Begin small, and then when you have critical mass, begin your large-group setting.

Focus on how to make Sunday school an event that children are sorry to miss. Is it exciting? Do they have a friend they'll miss? Are they engaged when they attend? Do they say "aww" in disappointment when their parents arrive? Showing up is not the goal! You are after children who show up motivated to learn and grow in their relationship with Christ.■

Take It Home

List all the negative and positive ways you are rewarded (such as getting the best seat) or punished (such as missing the start of the movie) for being on time or late this week. What most motivated you to be on time? Were you mostly rewarded or punished?

A Good Excuse

Every one of us has complained at one time or another about attending work or going to school. "But five to ten percent of kids dislike [school] so much they don't want to attend," says Christopher Kearney, director of the Child School Refusal and Anxiety Disorders Clinic at the University of Nevada, Las Vegas. A child could have several reasons for not wanting to attend school. According to Kearney, "these difficulties can be the result of specific fears, general anxiety, social anxiety, separation problems, attention-seeking problems, or family problems." Also, a child may have trouble with the teacher and would simply need to move to a different class.

It's time for a CHANGE

Lord, help me to encourage children to get excited about you and our class by…

SCRIPTURES to Study
Commit it to MEMORY

"Every day they continued to meet together in the temple courts."

—Acts 2:46a

■ What do you think would have made the early church want to meet every day?

■ What motivates you to attend church?

Who Said THAT?

"I planted the seed, Apollos watered it, but God made it grow."

—Paul (1 Corinthians 3:6)

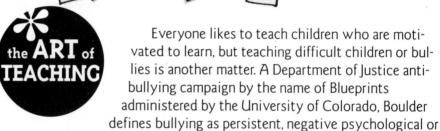

Well, I see that your class is ready to learn. Let me know if you need anything. I'll be at the church down the street.

Teaching Challenging Children

Think It Over

Both speed bumps and brick walls are made out of very hard material. Our response to these barriers will determine whether we wreck our cars or are merely inconvenienced. Your reaction to students who appear to have little desire to learn determines if they slow your classroom down, redirect it, or wreck it.

Man looks on the outside. God looks at the heart.

the ART of TEACHING

Everyone likes to teach children who are motivated to learn, but teaching difficult children or bullies is another matter. A Department of Justice anti-bullying campaign by the name of Blueprints administered by the University of Colorado, Boulder defines bullying as persistent, negative psychological or physical acts directed by a stronger student or group against a weaker one. Every day, according to the National Association of School Psychologists, 160,000 American young people skip school fearing they will be the targets of bullies. How can you create an environment where everyone learns even when you have bullies, smart alecks, or others who lack the motivation to learn in your classroom?

Begin by asking for help from those who are also involved with these students. The students' pastors, parents, friends, and previous teachers will give you some great advice on how to motivate the children. These partners in ministry may show you that you shouldn't work alone in your classroom. Perhaps the challenging child might benefit from a little personal attention from another teacher or parent.

If you find you need more help, try enlisting a mature adult who will give full-time help to the child as a project of compassion. One-on-one tutoring is only effective, however, if the child senses you are in it for the long term. Short-term solutions for a child who is undermotivated will only reinforce his or her worldview that no one cares.

Try to understand the child's motivation. The behavior is most likely rooted in emotional need. Look for ways to meet the child's needs while meeting the needs of your motivated learners. Work to make the child your ally by developing a relationship with the child. Help the child understand what you are trying to accomplish, and give him or her opportunities to help you succeed. Help the child see that he or she is an important part of your class, as the child may have experienced rejection in many other social situations.

Most important, use humor. Showing fear or insecurity around a bully will encourage his or her behavior. Experts say that humor is one way to stop bullies! It helps you maintain a sense of control while at the same time disarms anger or passive aggression. ■

Motivation

Bill Cosby, playing the role of Dr. Cliff Huxtable, was sitting at the dinner table with his daughter Rudy. Rudy refused to finish her dinner, and her father would not let her leave the table until she had finished her meal. Rudy refused to eat, so Cliff told the story about another five-year-old who would not finish her dinner. All her friends went to middle school, graduated from high school, and went to college, but the young girl remained at her dinner table. Rudy, apparently, was not impressed—she still would not finish her meal.

Denise, Rudy's older sister, came into the house, and Rudy could hear Denise and her friends move the living room couch, roll up the carpet, start to play music, and begin to dance. Just then, Denise came into the kitchen, and Rudy asked her older sister if she could join them. Denise said, "Sure, as soon as you finish your dinner."

Rudy ate her three brussels sprouts, placed the plate in the sink, and went out to dance.

SCRIPTURES to Study
* Commit it to MEMORY

"Carry each other's burdens, and in this way you will fulfill the law of Christ."
—Galatians 6:2

■ In what ways do we label children?

■ How can you effectively assess children without labeling them?

Take It Home

Take some time this week to approach the customer service counter at a department store where you frequently shop. You can either ask the counter staff about the angriest customer of the day or just stand back and watch the people who come up to try to get something done.

Ask the staff to tell you some strategies they use to calm down a customer or diffuse a volatile situation. Write down some of these to use in your classroom when faced with difficult kids.

It's time for a CHANGE

TIC... TOC... TIC...

Lord, help me reach those difficult children in my classroom or neighborhood by...

Who Said THAT?

"Bless me—me too, my father!"

—Esau, crying out to his father for a blessing after being tricked by his twin brother, Jacob (Genesis 27:34)

A Window of Opportunity

Think It Over

It has been called the 4/14 Window (a comparison to the 10/40 Window where 40 percent of the world's unreached people live in a 1-degree latitude at the equator stretching around the globe). The 4/14 Window is the period between the ages of four and fourteen when 60 percent of Christians come to a saving faith.

the ART of TEACHING

A survey by Barna Research reports that "Most of the people who accept Jesus Christ as their savior do so at a young age. The median is age 16. In total, six out of ten people say they made their decision to accept Christ before age 18."

As a teacher, there can be no greater joy than to see a young person say yes to Jesus' gift of eternal life.

For some, this is as easy as the most natural conversation. For others, it is a dreaded talk that rivals our deepest fear. What do you need to succeed in helping a child become a Christian?

Like so many things in God's kingdom, helping others find Christ starts with love. Love those who do not know Christ! There is a children's ministry leader in Florida who, prior to praying for the meal, asks the waiter or waitress if there is anything special the church staff could remember in prayer. A church in Texas takes one Sunday a month to present a clear call for children to become Christians.

It's important to understand that we don't save; God does. It is not the cleverness of our words that produces results; it is the work of the Holy Spirit! We can't take credit when our lessons help children grow or when they lead the unchurched to faith in Jesus. It is God at work in us, working for his good pleasure. With that said, try to share Christ's love in *every* lesson. You will find that children can make Jesus their *forever friend* at the end of a lesson on David and Goliath just as easily as after a lesson on Christ dying on the cross.

Finally, understand how God saves us. God created a sinless creation for his good pleasure. But all of us have sinned and come short of the glory of God. Since God cannot have sin near him, we are separated from God. But the good news is that God sent his own Son, Jesus Christ, to die on our behalf to pay for our sin. Children need to put their faith in Jesus to receive his forgiveness! ∎

Come and Get It

I had the privilege of helping the evangelist Franklin Graham present the Gospel message to children around the world. In Kingston, Jamaica, Franklin was coached to say to children at the crusade, "If you made a decision to make Jesus your forever friend, we want to talk to you. Come down here onto the field and a 'big' person will help if you have any questions." I mentioned that we should definitely *not* say, "Come down here onto the field and a big person will *give* you something," because the entire stadium would run onto the field. Well, that Saturday morning, sure enough, Franklin used the magic words that caused nearly 7,000 children to not just walk forward—they ran to get whatever the "big person" had to give them!

SCRIPTURES to Study
*Commit it to MEMORY

"For God so loved the world that he gave his one and only Son, that whoever believes in him shall not perish but have eternal life."

—John 3:16

■ How is your belief today different from when you first became a Christian?

■ How would you describe eternal life?

Take It Home

Reflect on your own faith journey. Write down the major events or circumstances that helped you become a Christian, and make note of the events that helped you continue in faith. Realizing that different Christians have different experiences that brought them to Christ, think about how God can use your experience to help non-Christians.

It's time for a CHANGE

Lord, bring one person into my life this week with whom I can share my own faith story. Help me begin by...

Who Said THAT?

"For the greatest and most regal work of God is the salvation of humanity."

—Saint Clement of Alexandria, *Paedagogus*

It Takes Two to ~~Tango~~ Teach!

Think It Over

Open conflict, hidden agendas, and passive aggression all contribute to an unhealthy classroom. Your interactions with team members speak more loudly to children than what you say. How healthy is your team?

the ART of TEACHING

Several teaching teams arrived at the training meeting. One group was having the time of its life. These three teachers had been together for the past three years. They were having fun, were fun for the kids, and were fun to watch. Another team had one veteran and four brand-new recruits who were full of questions for their leader. Other groups were in various stages of connection. One group of five teachers was very, very quiet. They were each reading new teacher guides, and not one of them ventured to say a word to the others.

We can no longer teach alone even if we wanted to. Safety demands that there are two adults with children at all times. Since team dynamics are an inevitable (and beneficial) aspect of children's ministry, it's important to consider elements of effective teamwork. What can you do to create a sense of team harmony?

It's important that your team has a leader. Perhaps there is a designated leader or a natural leader has risen to the top. It is critical that there is someone on your team who takes ultimate responsibility for the team and makes the final call on tough decisions. Every team needs a leader who is in charge of assigning roles and responsibilities as well as helping mismatched volunteers grow into their roles or move on to new responsibilities. Classrooms run efficiently to the extent that people work according to their gifts and interests. Effective team leaders encourage dialogue and discussion, and effective team members support their leader.

Leaders and members alike must work to communicate routinely outside of the classroom. You can encourage a sense of teamwork and unity by connecting during the week. Communication should be characterized by open, direct, consistent, and honest feedback. Don't seek out conflict, but don't avoid it. In fact, every functioning team will experience conflict at some level. Commit to one another that you will work through the conflict together. You'll find that your relationships, teamwork, and effectiveness are always strengthened after successfully navigating disagreements or hurt feelings.

Finally, if your team is not functioning well, ask for help from your children's ministry leader to consult with the team or to help the team navigate conflict. At the very worst, ask to be reassigned rather than resigning! There is a place for you and a team for you to work with—just give it time! ∎

Back to the Basics

Just before a key NFL game, Vince Lombardi, probably the most inspiring coach in the history of the game of football, speaks to his players about teamwork.

"And now," coach says, "I want you, all of you, to know this. Regardless of what happens today this is a team of which I am proud. Regardless of the outcome today I'll still be proud of you. To win, though, you're going to have to run harder and tackle harder and block harder. It's going to take a great team effort, so let's have it! Let's go!"

"Let's go!" the team stands and shouts. They won, 9–7!

—From *Run to Daylight* by Vince Lombardi, with W.C. Heinz

SCRIPTURES *to Study*

✱ Commit it to MEMORY

"Carry each other's burdens, and in this way you will fulfill the law of Christ."

—Galatians 6:2

■ How have you carried someone else's burdens?

■ How have your burdens been carried by someone else?

■ What stops you from asking for help?

Take It Home

Buy a puzzle that has around fifty pieces. This week invite your team over to your house for prayer and planning. Begin your time by saying, "We are going to work on a quick project together." Then, without showing team members the puzzle picture on the box, spread out the pieces to see how quickly you can put them together. After some confusion and even questions such as "Hey, where's the box?" pull out the box and retry putting the puzzle together. Ask:

■ What were the differences in putting the puzzle together with and without the picture?

■ How is that like or unlike our current vision for our team and our classroom?

It's time for a CHANGE

Lord, help me value the strengths of others by...

Who Said THAT?

"Coming together is a beginning, keeping together is progress, working together is success."

—Henry Ford

Effective Small Groups

She's not going to take an offering, is she?

Think It Over

Jesus spoke to crowds that numbered more than 5,000. However, Jesus called only twelve to follow him. The twelve even became his friends. What does Jesus' style of leadership say about how we should teach children?

the ART of TEACHING

My first Sunday school classroom experience was with a small group of third-grade boys. We sat around a table each Sunday and waited until everyone was settled. The lead teacher handed me a pre-session paper activity that was to be completed before I led my boys into the main room for "large group" story time. We found that the pre-session paperwork was finished off in short order. The boys wanted to talk—and we did. By the second month of this routine, the pre-session activity became just a doodle pad. We had important things to share!

According to the University of Minnesota, children in small groups are more cooperative, respond better to the caregiver, and are more likely to participate in activities than they are in a large group of children. Simply setting up small groups doesn't ensure better learning. Several skills are necessary to improve your ability to connect with your small group and create a safe environment in which spiritual growth can take place.

Small group leaders must be good listeners. Ears *and* eyes hear! A little girl asked one teacher a question. The teacher continued looking over the girl while responding with an affirmative "Uh-huh." The little girl immediately grabbed the teacher's face and reprimanded, "Wissen to me!" Make eye contact with the children in your small group, and show them that you're interested in what they have to say—and *really* listen to their thoughts, feelings, and ideas.

One of the most important elements of small group dynamics is the group size. Healthy small-group size is relative to how much you and the group can handle. If you have a child in your small group who has significant emotional or learning needs, you'll probably need to have fewer children in your group. Small groups with four to seven children offer the greatest opportunities for discussion and inclusion.

Including everyone and encouraging participation are the leader's most important responsibilities. Do you notice how some children hang back and don't talk while others love to talk? Pull quiet children close to you to make them feel as much a part of the group as those who are more gregarious. Look for opportunities to bring quiet or shy children into the conversation. When they choose to participate, look for opportunities to help them shine.

Make certain each child is a valued member of the group by assigning roles. Do you have someone who loves to read? Another who loves to help set out supplies? One who loves to collect prayer requests? And another who loves to pray? Social interrelationships nurture security and foster community in the classroom! ∎

Look through the TV guide or the top ten TV shows as measured by Nielsen Media Research, and highlight all the evening programs that portray groups in some form or another. What is the proportion between shows that feature a loner or couple and those that feature a group of three or more? What does this tell you about what the studio executives feel people want? What TV show does your classroom most resemble from this list?

Tell a Friend

The great evangelist Billy Graham is a wonderful speaker and a great Christian. Graham relies on one key ingredient to fill stadiums: small groups of people! Operation Andrew was devised in the late 1950s after the hugely successful London, England crusade. People came out in droves to hear this American through invitations from friends who heard a message of hope. Operation Andrew was named after Andrew in the Bible. Andrew was one of the first disciples called by Jesus to come and follow him. "The first thing Andrew did was to find his brother Simon [Peter] and tell him, 'We have found the Messiah' (that is, the Christ). And he brought him to Jesus" (John 1:41-42a).

SCRIPTURES to Study
* Commit it to MEMORY

"Follow my example, as I follow the example of Christ."
—1 Corinthians 11:1

■ Who was the person you most wanted to be like while growing up?

■ How would a small group help your children learn about your example as a Christian better than a large group?

TIC... TOC... TIC...
It's time for a
CHANGE

Help me to listen and know my students by not...

Help me to lead and understand my students by...

Who Said THAT?

"You cannot confront someone you do not have a relationship with."

—Howard Hendricks

The Unsung Heroes

Think It Over

We couldn't do it without the unsung heroes! Behind-the-scenes work is often done in obscurity and anonymity. When was the last time you thanked the person who helps you do your job?

the ART of TEACHING

From record keeping to purchasing supplies, the unsung heroes of the classroom are the helpers and administrators. Without their diligent help, teachers and small group leaders would not be able to do what they do best. But these servants tend to be overlooked, under-appreciated, and often ignored because of their desire for anonymity.

Thank you, helpers! Is it hard for you to accept praise and compliments? Saying "thank you" when you are complimented is helpful for you and for the person encouraging you. Try not to deny another person the reward of encouragement, while at the same time acknowledge the humility of accepting thanks!

Teachers and small-group leaders: Remember your helpers! Include them in your plans, your goals, and your celebrations. Take a moment to write them thank you notes, leave voice-mail messages of thanks, or send "Happy for No Occasion" gifts that you know they'll love. Give them a day off, encourage them, and thank them. Remember, someone with the gift of administration is harder on himself or herself than you ever could be. So when you need to correct them, do so delicately. ∎

No Lone Rangers

The first trip to the moon saw three men rocket beyond the boundaries of the earth's atmosphere to guide their lunar module to the surface of the moon. Neil Armstrong relayed those memorable words as his feet hit the dusty surface first: "That's one small step for a man, one giant leap for mankind." Armstrong and Buzz Aldrin planted the flag on the moon. Often forgotten are the unsung heroes at mission control in Houston, who guided the astronauts safely there and back. But the one person who had the most thankless job was perhaps Michael Collins, who had to orbit around the moon while the two other astronauts walked on the surface of the moon. The success of the few depended on the sacrifices of so many!

"The eye cannot say to the hand, 'I don't need you!' And the head cannot say to the feet, 'I don't need you!' "

—1 Corinthians 12:21

■ What helps you avoid envy, bitterness, or pity?

■ How can you encourage those with whom you work?

This week, write a note or two of thanks for those people who make your work at church much easier and more joyful. You might thank the pastor who shares the Word of God with you, the administrator who hands you the roll sheet, the greeter at the door, or even the Sunday school superintendent who worries about the details. Show how you value their contributions by pointing out specifically what they do to help you personally!

Help my heart stay humble by...

"Service...is love in action."

—Sarah Patton Boyle, U.S. Civil Rights activist and author

How Do I Use Curriculum?

Think It Over

The success of your classroom time is one-third content, one-third passion and attitude, and three-thirds dependence on the Holy Spirit!

the ART of TEACHING

I love the opening line to Dr. Spock's 1960s primer on child rearing. His opening advice to parents? "You know more than you think you do." The same holds true for teachers. Trust your instincts, you know more than you think you do about teaching!

One pastor was passing by a classroom of fifth-graders and noticed the teacher reading out of the teacher's guide to the children. The pastor was so troubled by the sterile teaching method that he found the Christian Education Pastor and asked that the teacher be removed. The CE Pastor listened calmly but reassured his boss that the teacher was a good communicator who must have been having a bad morning.

There are two equal and opposite errors of using any graded curriculum in your classroom. Teachers can rigidly follow the script while ignoring their own unique interests or the students' innate desires. This error can create a climate in which learning is stifled. Teachers can also ignore the curriculum altogether or wing a lesson that they've just casually read. This error creates the opposite danger of tangential, boring, and unfocused teaching. Here is some trust-your-instinct advice that will help you guide your students on any given Sunday.

Read quickly through your entire lesson once on Sunday afternoon (or after you finish your last lesson). Then take a break for a few days. You'll be amazed at what God will teach you while you let this lesson "incubate" in your own heart. Some lessons even offer a Bible Background section to assist you in personalizing the lesson before you teach it. Prepare your supplies for each activity before you teach the lesson. When children are working or involved in an activity, look ahead in your lesson or outline to determine what you need to do to transition to the next activity. Always stay a step or two in front of the kids so you can lead them.

Don't hesitate to make sure your classroom is arranged to complement your curriculum. This should be done on a regular basis, even if the room is a multiuse classroom or you are just there once a month. As you prepare your lessons, think about where you'll do each activity and the logistics of pulling it off. Make modifications for your needs and environment. For example, if a curriculum calls for a game of Tag and your class meets in a room the size of a cubicle, you can have children walk heel-to-toe or on their knees.

Look for places to add instruction on distinctives that are important to your church and denomination. Most curriculum publishers provide a great foundation for your lessons by focusing on the major aspects of the faith. They also avoid controversial topics such as methods of baptism and beliefs about communion. Your curriculum can serve as a great launching point for you to include the doctrines and practices that are important to your church.

Finally, don't be afraid to try things that you normally would avoid. For example, just because you hate drama or crafts doesn't mean the children in your class hate it. Give new ideas a good chance to succeed by making minor adjustments that fit your class. If you teach an activity with a bad attitude or with low enthusiasm, the activity is doomed from the start. ∎

That's Change!

Congratulate that pencil in your drawer. It will write as well in fifty years as it does today. But according to the National Center for State Courts, computer technology is changing so rapidly that some systems can become obsolete even before they're fully implemented.

SCRIPTURES to Study
Commit it to MEMORY

"May the words of my mouth and the meditation of my heart be pleasing in your sight, O Lord, my Rock and my Redeemer."

—Psalm 19:14

■ Why would the psalmist combine mouth and heart as areas of concern?

■ Which area above is your strength? Which area above is your weakness?

It's time for a **CHANGE**

Lord, let the words of my mouth and the meditations of my heart...

Step back and look at your next lesson from another angle. How do you define success in the classroom? This week choose one of the following activities to see curriculum in action.

■ Visit an elementary school or another church, and spend the morning with the age level you teach. Ask to see the teacher's lesson plan prior to the start of the visit so you can get acquainted with what his or her goals are.

■ Visit an experimental or teaching day-care center at the local community college or university. Often, new techniques and research are done at these facilities. You may also see state-of-the-art equipment that creates an environment in which learning is enhanced.

■ Visit an unusual learning facility such as a day care attached to a casino (seriously!) or one at a corporate headquarters. The point here is to see money-is-no-object in action.

Who Said THAT?

"One looks back with appreciation to the brilliant teachers, but with gratitude to those who touched our human feelings. The curriculum is so much necessary raw material, but warmth is the vital element for the growing plant and for the soul of the child."

—Carl Jung, Swiss psychiatrist

 Published in *Teacher Training on the Go* by Group Publishing, Inc., P.O. Box 481, Loveland, CO 80539. www.grouppublishing.com

Emotional Safety

Sometimes I don't want anyone to talk at me.

Think It Over

There is a lot of discussion about safety in the classroom. Criminal background checks, antibacterial soap, the "two-adult rule," and windows on every classroom have become the norm. Physical safety is essential. But emotional safety is also essential if kids are going to open up and connect. Is your classroom emotionally safe?

the ART of TEACHING

Have you ever asked a question in class only to receive blank stares and fidgets? Children stare down at the ground, look at you with crinkled brows, or begin talking about something that's completely unrelated. When kids don't connect, we often attribute it to a lack of interest or focus. But the problem could be that they just don't feel safe to share.

If you don't care about your children's feelings or passions and are only interested in what they know, you will connect only with part of who they are. If you want emotional connections, you must look for ways to facilitate them. Simple factors such as environment go a long way in affecting emotional safety. The way a classroom is arranged can impede sharing. A classroom where everyone is on the floor in a circle makes sharing much easier than one where children are lined up in tables and chairs.

Look directly into the eyes of each child as he or she speaks. Show active and empathetic listening through your body language by leaning forward, keeping your arms from crossing, and nodding your head. The quickest and easiest way to show that your classroom is not a safe place for emotions is to judge, evaluate, or correct a child's feelings. If a child holds a belief that is heretical or wrong, affirm his or her willingness to share and gently offer points of clarification that line up with Scripture and sound thinking.

Some children need time to open up. A child's home-life may prevent the child from sharing his or her feelings on a regular basis. You may not see the immediate effects of the safe environment you've created. The child may begin to share later in life or just before he or she moves on to another class. Discipleship is a process in which you have only a small part. Don't expect to reap all the benefits this year.

Work to avoid talking when faced with silence. Children need time to formulate their responses. What seems like an eternity to a waiting questioner is often not enough time for a child who is thinking about his or her answer. If you persist in pausing after a question and waiting for a response, one will come in time. Show your smile as you wait, and express delight when children respond! ∎

Water

That's Communication!—

The story of Helen Keller and Anne Sullivan is a poignant reminder of a patient teacher finally breaking through to a blind and deaf six-year-old girl.

At a plain well pump, a "miracle" took place. Miss Sullivan was pumping cool water into one of Helen's hands while tapping out an alphabet code of five letters in the other hand, first slowly, then rapidly. Helen struggled as Miss Sullivan tried again and again. Suddenly, the signals crossed Helen's mind with a meaning. She knew that "w-a-t-e-r" meant the cool something flowing over her hand. By that evening, Helen had learned thirty words. After four months of instruction, Helen knew four hundred words, not counting the numerous proper nouns!

Take It Home

The next time you are in a class or a small group, watch how the leader facilitates discussion. What did the leader do to make people feel safe or unsafe to share their thoughts and feelings? During the class or meeting, make a mental note of things you would like to do differently to provide a safe emotional environment for your kids.

SCRIPTURES to Study
Commit it to MEMORY

"But we were gentle among you, like a mother caring for her little children. We loved you so much that we were delighted to share with you not only the gospel of God but our lives as well, because you had become so dear to us."

—1 Thessalonians 2:7-8

■ With which children in your classroom have you become like a "mother"?

■ How have they responded?

It's time for a CHANGE

God, help me parent my Sunday school class better by...

Who Said THAT?

"No pessimist ever discovered the secret of the stars, or sailed to an uncharted land, or opened a new doorway for the human spirit."

—Helen Keller

Finishing Well: When to Say "When"

Think It Over

The time is coming for you to decide if you would like to return to the classroom. Saying yes is often pretty easy. But how can you know when to say no and how to say it?

the ART of TEACHING

God's call for us to serve in a specific area is not always a permanent assignment. It can be, and most often is, a season of service. You are not married to the ministry, but you do have a commitment to fulfill. Your decision to quit is ultimately between you and the Lord. While it is wise to seek counsel, too many chefs spoil the soup. God will give you peace about your decision. And remember, guilt is not a God-given guide. Here are some guidelines on how to gracefully say no to service without saying no to God!

Pray and ask God where you should serve. You have been "created in Christ Jesus to do good works" (Ephesians 2:10) and have been given gifts and talents to use in the church. You cannot *not* serve. If you say no to children's ministry, you need to say yes somewhere else!

Before you say no, remember your first love. Why did you say yes in the first place? Perhaps you didn't know what you were getting into, or maybe you're not gifted to serve children. Maybe you simply need to be retrained, re-motivated, and re-energized. Let your leader know you need help! Solid leadership will always advocate for the person, not the position.

Finally, take your time! If you feel disagreeable, wait to say no. Don't abandon ship at the first sign of trouble or after the first lesson that bombs. Often our failures or perceived inadequacies are thinly disguised opportunities for God to show *his* power and *his* pleasure in us!

If you're certain that God is calling you elsewhere, work out an exit strategy with your leader. It's unfair and unrighteous to quit the night before you're supposed to teach. Set a definite date that allows your leader ample time to find a replacement. Just as you need to serve faithfully until that date, your leader needs to honor the commitment to let you go at that time. Finish well by working with your leader to help find, recruit, and train your replacement. ■

Make It Worthwhile

A Bruskin/Goldring Research survey sponsored by the UPS Foundation asked veteran volunteers why they quit. Forty percent said they stopped volunteering because the organization wasted their time. Interestingly, these complaints ranked second to "time pressures." Sixty-five percent of volunteers stated they stopped because of personal time pressure. Only 10 percent said they stopped because "they were not thanked."

SCRIPTURES to Study
*Commit it to MEMORY

"We have different gifts, according to the grace given us. If a man's gift is prophesying, let him use it in proportion to his faith. If it is serving, let him serve; if it is teaching, let him teach; if it is encouraging, let him encourage; if it is contributing to the needs of others, let him give generously; if it is leadership, let him govern diligently; if it is showing mercy, let him do it cheerfully."

—Romans 12:6-8

■ What is the connection between having a gift and using it?

■ How have you been using your gift?

Take It Home

This week pray honestly about your commitment this past season and listen for God's answer.

Try one of the following to gain insight into what you should do next.

■ Take your child, your spouse, or a friend out on a date. As the main topic of conversation, talk about whether or not you should continue to serve.

■ Open your Bible to the passage in which God meets Moses at the burning bush and encourages him to volunteer. Think about how Moses' journey is similar to your situation.

It's time for a CHANGE

Lord, serving is not easy, and leading sometimes is not a joy. Restore the joy of my teaching...

Help me find my place in your church by...

Who Said THAT?

"No sacrifice is worth the name unless it is a joy. Sacrifice and a long face go ill together."

—Mohandas K. Gandhi, *Young India*

... And in conclusion...

SERVICE 10:30

Let Us Worship

Think It Over

the ART of TEACHING

Worshipping God is like drinking water. Are you coming into class after drinking from a dripping faucet or an open fire hydrant?

"Praise God from whom all blessings flow..."

We know that worship is important in connecting our hearts to God. Some feel that children can only worship with their parents in a worship service. Others feel compelled to replicate the "big church" feel for kids in a large-group setting. Children can most certainly engage in worship. But helping children worship is not bound to specific models or methodology. How can you spend more time in worship and help kids find that same connection?

To help children engage in worship, look closely at your own life. As you sing praises with children, are you just leading music or worshipping? Whether or not you "play" the stereo or the piano, you're actions are telling children something. Praise is a prayer to God with music accompaniment. When you lead children, you're looking to God—not at the tops of the kids' heads.

One four-year-old was leaving a message on the answering machine for his father at work. Unwittingly, he said, "Daddy? I want you to know that I will be playing across the street at Matt's house when you get home. In Jesus' name I pray, amen." Even when children cannot see us, they know we are real. Children can also understand that they are praying to a God who is really there even if they don't see him!

However, they might not completely understand why they sing praises to God or what they should expect or do while singing. Give opportunities for children to express what praising God means to them and why they sing praises. Tell children what praising God means to you. Continually remind children that praising God means singing to him with their hearts rather than just singing about God. Provide opportunities for children to sing rambunctious songs with high-energy motions and quiet songs with no motions at all. Help your kids understand that both kinds of song give opportunities for real worship.

Help children see that worship goes beyond singing. A well-prepared responsive reading can be surprisingly meaningful for young readers. Times of silent prayer and reflection can lead children to connect directly with God. Most important, help children see that worship goes beyond the classroom or church. They can worship during a hike and even during a test! Help children see that everything they do can be an act of worship to their loving God. ■

Take It Home

Often we get so lulled into a particular type of worship experience that we forget what children go through as they learn how to worship. This week choose one of the following activities:

■ Attend a Sunday evening or Saturday evening worship service at a church that is of a different denomination and, therefore, a different worshipping tradition. Ask yourself, "How does the 'style' of worship impact my own experience and connection with God?"

■ Attend a prayer or worship service that is held at a rest home, a prison, a rescue mission, or even an airport. Ask yourself, "What happens when a variety of people come together for a common experience? How does this impact my own experience?"

What Is Worship?

According to Barna Research, "the most likely definitions [of *worship*] held by people related to expressions of praise or thanks to God (19%); praying to God (17%); attending church services (17%); having a personal relationship with God (12%); a particular attitude toward God (10%); or a way of living that reflects one's spiritual commitment (9%)." Also according to Barna Research, "nearly two-thirds of regular attenders say they have never experienced God's presence at a church service."

It's time for a CHANGE

Lord, help my work for you to never replace my worship of you. Help me free up time this week to worship you by...

SCRIPTURES to Study
* Commit it to MEMORY

"Worship the Lord with gladness; come before him with joyful songs."

—Psalm 100:2

■ How, other than with gladness, can you come before God?

■ When have you felt the closest to God?

■ What can you do or where should you go to feel close to God again?

Who Said THAT?

"It is only when men begin to worship that they begin to grow."

—Calvin Coolidge

Dealing With Difficult Subjects

I find this is the best way to deal with problems in the classroom.

Think It Over

The only difficult subjects in the Sunday school classroom are subjects for which you are not prepared.

the ART of TEACHING

This class of boys was notorious for trying to test the patience of their teacher, but the teacher was always prepared with a great response. Trying to fluster his teacher, a fifth-grader asked, "What is circumcision?" The teacher gave the medically correct answer without blinking an eye! In a different class, another teacher overheard one sweet girl sharing about her father and his problem with drugs. Elsewhere, a young boy asked the teacher, "How come Madison doesn't have a dad?"

Surprising questions happen for a reason. God created children to be curious. Curiosity is a virtue that compels a child to ask, explore, learn, and ultimately grow. Try not to stifle questions with a grimace, knee-jerk response, or other demeaning reaction.

If you don't know the answer or how you should respond, work to gather more information to see what the child already understands and what he or she is truly trying to understand. Words and phrases such as "Really?" "Please tell me more," and "What do you think?" will help you stall while *you* think and give you more information with which to respond.

Be thankful for these tough questions! The alternative is often silence or misunderstanding. If you encounter tough questions, congratulations! You've succeeded in piquing their interest and awakening their curiosity. According to *Webster's New World College Dictionary, curiosity* means a "desire to learn or know." There's no need to motivate an already engaged child who wants to know something and learn!

Sometimes a child just needs to share his or her feelings. Children need to process their heartaches. Questioning is often the means of doing just that. Listen uncritically, respond gracefully, and look to God to provide the answer by stopping to pray for that child out loud! ■

Reacting to Tragedy

The following is the letter sent to elementary school children the day after 9/11 by the first lady, Laura Bush.

September 12, 2001
Dear Children:

Many Americans were injured or lost their lives in the recent national tragedy. All their friends and loved ones are feeling very sad, and you may be feeling sad, frightened, or confused, too.

I want to reassure you that many people—including your family, your teachers, and your school counselor—love and care about you and are looking out for your safety. You can talk with them and ask them questions. You can also write down your thoughts or draw a picture that shows how you are feeling and share that with the adults in your life.

When sad or frightening things happen, all of us have an opportunity to become better people by thinking about others. We can show them we care about them by saying so and by doing nice things for them. Helping others will make you feel better, too.

I want you to know how much I care about all of you. Be kind to each other, take care of each other, and show your love for each other.

With best wishes,
Laura Bush

Take It Home

This week, stop by a pediatrician's office or a school counselor's office and request information on topics that affect you and your students. Topics could include sex, resolving conflict, divorce, terrorism, drugs and alcohol, and pollution.

It's time for a CHANGE

Lord, help me be prepared to respond to the children I care for when they ask questions by...

SCRIPTURES to Study
Commit it to MEMORY

"Then he opened their minds so they could understand the Scriptures."

—Luke 24:45

■ How has your mind been opened lately in understanding the Bible?

■ How can you help your students understand this verse?

Who Said THAT?

"Curiosity is one of the most permanent and certain characteristics of a vigorous intellect."

—Samuel Johnson, *The Rambler*

Time Management for Maximum Teaching

Lord, there has to be a better way!

Think It Over

SPARE TIME?

In the course of a week, we have 168 hours to spend. This is a fixed amount that every person has (unless he or she is on an airplane crossing time zones where he or she could lose or gain an hour or two). If you sleep eight hours a night, that's fifty-six hours a week. If you work full time, you spend at least forty hours on the job. If you spend an hour for each meal, then you spend 21 hours per week eating. If you spend two hours a day cleaning, cooking, and doing yard work, that's fourteen hours per week. If you spend an hour going to and from your job, then you use seven hours per week in your car. That leaves thirty hours of leisure time that you have in a given week to shower, shop, watch TV, attend church, read, play, or study for next week's lesson!

the **ART** of **TEACHING**

Albert Einstein, the great physicist who theorized that time was relative, tried to explain the theory of relativity with the following: "When you are courting a nice girl an hour seems like a second. When you sit on a red-hot cinder a second seems like an hour. That's relativity."

As a Sunday school teacher, Saturday afternoon leaves an eternity ahead to plan a lesson, gather supplies, call students, and set up the classroom. After all, stores are open to make that last-minute purchase, the kids are playing outside, and your spouse is busy on that project which will leave you uninterrupted time to prepare. Wait until Saturday evening, and time compels stores to close and spouses and children to interrupt your thoughts with their needs.

Your experience will tell you how much time you need. Everyone needs different amounts of time to prepare. Experience can shorten the time needed. Anxiety can lengthen the time required. Your expectations will tell you how much time you need. If you are a perfectionist, there is not enough time in a week to get it right. If you are a freer spirit, more in awe of whimsy than logic, you will have more than enough time while you put on your makeup in the car on the way to church to prepare your lesson.

Your results will tell you how much time you need in the future. Unfortunately, by the time you realize what you've done, it's too late. But the best way to measure results is one week at a time. Did the craft go too quickly? Was the lesson understood in half the time? Did the kids breeze through the questions? Should you have spent more time in the Bible exploration activity that had everyone laughing with excitement?

Your faith journey will tell you how much time you need. Don't overlook the fact that as you prepare to teach, and even when you are in the act of teaching, *you will be changed*! The teacher always learns more than the student. The time you spend on your lesson will add to the richness of what God is saying to you and through you. Allow enough time in your preparation for your personal growth.

Take a look at the lesson early in the week so you understand how much time your lesson planning will take. If you start the week with a strong understanding of your topic, you can look for connections and pick up supplies throughout the week. Last-minute planning limits your effectiveness. If you think of a great video clip to use on Saturday night, you probably won't be able to rent it, preview it, and prepare to use it by Sunday morning. However, if the idea crosses your mind on Monday, you can pick up the movie on the way home from work during the week. With a little forethought, preparing for your lessons can actually be an enjoyable and enriching time rather than a harried, panicked drain. ■

SUN: afternoon, read over next lesson
MON: pray for/call/send card to those absent
TUES: pray for each child in class, memorize Bible verse
WED: pick up needed supplies
THURS: in-depth Bible lesson study, highlight vital points
FRI: go over lesson out loud
SAT: assemble notes, crafts, take-home papers
SUN: arrive in class early to set up

It Keeps Tickin'

Imagine you had a bank that credited your account each morning with $86,000. That amount carried over no balance from day to day, allowed you to keep no cash in your account, and every evening cancelled whatever part of the amount you failed to use during the day. What would you do? Draw out every cent every day, of course, and use it to your advantage! Well, you have such a bank, and its name is *time*! Every morning it credits you with 86,400 seconds. Every night it rules off as lost whatever of this you failed to invest to good purpose. It carries over no balances, and it allows no overdrafts. Each day it opens a new account with you. If you fail to use the day's deposits, the loss is yours. There is no going back. There is no drawing against tomorrow.

SCRIPTURES *to Study*
✳ Commit it to MEMORY

"Teach us to number our days aright, that we may gain a heart of wisdom."
—Psalm 90:12

■ What does it feel like to you when you number your days?

■ What keeps you from numbering your days?

Take It Home

Create a schedule for your lesson preparation, and follow it for three weeks. Make adjustments based on your own personal style. Write down the "new-and-improved" schedule on a piece of paper, and staple it to your teacher's guide. Don't forget to share your observations with your co-workers at your next team meeting!

TIC... TOC... TIC...

It's time for a CHANGE

God, help me to use the time you give me by...

Who Said THAT?

"Time is the coin of your life. It is the only coin you have, and only you can determine how it will be spent. Be careful lest you let other people spend it for you."

—Carl Sandburg

Puppets, Felt, and Other Fuzzy Memories

Think It Over

"Over 110 million children, the majority of them girls, are not in school—while countless others lack qualified teachers and even pencils and paper."

—Carol Bellamy, Executive Director of UNICEF, in an address to the ARCO Forum at Harvard's Institute of Politics, February 19, 2003.

the ART of TEACHING

Have you ever wondered what makes a child want to play with a refrigerator box instead of some other more expensive toy? Why are children drawn to blank sheets of paper as opposed to our intricate coloring sheets? Creativity and imagination are powerful motivators for children. There are many low-tech options that you can use to spark creativity in a child, save money, and enhance learning for children.

Puppets have been entertaining and instructing children in nearly every culture since ancient times. Using puppets can successfully reinforce your lesson while adding flair and fun. You can develop your own puppet team or simply have children make their own puppets and act out the lesson they just read or heard. Children can prepare presentations for the entire congregation, or you can have older children stage a performance for the younger children in your church.

Flannel can be fun! Think of flannel as a one-dimensional puppet that can be used to reinforce a lesson. You may have bad memories of being bored to tears as you watched your teacher tell the story on a flannel board. You can create different sorts of memories for the kids in your class by allowing them to get involved in the story. Let children help create, touch, and teach with the flannel. The best things about flannel are that it's simple to create, reusable, and can be an effective learning tool.

Does the thought of using chalk in your classroom make the hair on your neck bristle like nails on a chalkboard? Chalk isn't much fun if you're watching the teacher write on a blackboard. But bringing in color and putting chalk in the hands of children can transform your blackboard or sidewalk into a work of art dedicated to the glory of God that can rival the Sistine Chapel. Have children create scenes from your Bible story as you tell it or create pictures of what the story means to them. Chalk is a simple tool to widen the canvas of your storytelling.

You may have thrown out low-tech teaching tools because you feel that today's media-savvy children will find the old methods too boring. You'll find that with a little creativity and forethought, the exact opposite is true. You can use low-tech tools for high-impact lessons by involving children and providing new experiences. There are many more low-tech methods for teaching, such as ink stamps, feathers, stickers, puzzles, play tattoos, gardening, live animals, games, and toys. The tool is much less important than the way you use it. Remember, the worst way to teach is the way you always teach. Use what you have to make things fresh and new every week. ■

Reality Check

What is the difference between countries that have a lot of resources and those that do not? According to UNICEF's 2001 "State of the World's Children" report:

■ There are 23 televisions per 1,000 people in undeveloped nations; 641 in developed nations.

■ Sixty-one percent of primary students reach grades five in undeveloped nations compared to 99 percent in industrialized countries.

■ The GNP is $261 per family in undeveloped nations compared to $26,157 in industrialized countries.

Local craft stores are great places to look for simple supplies you can use to help your children learn. Many of the supplies are new variations on old classics (such as changeable markers). Visit a craft store to browse for possibilities or sign up for the next class that will help you make a craft that you've never made before.

It's time for a CHANGE

Help me keep my words simple so that your message will be powerful. Help me to change my teaching by...

SCRIPTURES to Study
Commit it to MEMORY

"To the weak I became weak, to win the weak. I have become all things to all men so that by all possible means I might save some."

—1 Corinthians 9:22

■ What "weaknesses" in your classroom or children's ministry can you turn into opportunities to reach your kids?

■ How can you make the most of the tools God has given you?

Who Said THAT?

"Why, a four-year-old child could understand this report. Run out and get me a four-year-old child."

—Groucho Marx, in the movie *Duck Soup*

Bringing Faith Home

I can't remember what we learned today.

Think It Over

Research shows that the home is the primary place of faith development for children. How does your children's ministry empower parents to shape their children's faith? How do you involve parents in ministering to their children?

the ART of TEACHING

How connected are you to the parents of the children you instruct? Do you view them as innocent bystanders—thankful for your service but largely ignorant of your work, successes, and failures in teaching their children? Or do you view them as essential partners in your effort to instruct, inspire, and promote Christlike character. The power and influence of the home is too strong and important to think we can minister effectively without including parents. Children, families, and teachers benefit when we work with families to reach their children.

Discipline problems are often eliminated when parents are kept informed of their child's success in the classroom. Who knows a child better than his or her family? Parents can give you strategies, insights, and solutions for their children that include knowledge of experiences and personalities that you've only begun to see. Diffuse defensive reactions to your requests for insight by asking parents to help you make the learning experience more beneficial and enjoyable for their children. By connecting with parents, you develop a more complete understanding of the child in your care. You'll learn why Lucy is so quiet or why Carlos doesn't handle transitions well if you listen to parents or even see their own lives up close.

To partner with parents, consider holding an open house! Allow parents to look into your classroom by having children bring their parents to class. You can also connect by e-mailing, writing, or calling parents with updates and stories from the classroom. Minister to parents by making observations regarding the positive growth you see in their children. You can give to parents general monthly prayer requests and specific prayer requests regarding spiritual goals you have for the individual child. Reach out to parents by acknowledging them and their children in the hallways, in "big church," or at the grocery store when you meet them. If the child's parents are not connected to your faith community, you will help them see the benefit of a caring church in your own sensitive attention to their child. ■

Family Power

Barna Research notes that 63 percent of parents who attended church as children will bring their own children to church. Compare that to only 33 percent of parents who themselves never attended church as children and now bring their children.

Take It Home

This week, instead of working on a section of the lesson yourself, call the parents of one of your children to see if they would be willing to either lead a short section or bring supplies that will be used in that section. For extra credit, enlist two families to work together to prepare that section of the lesson you assign.

It's time for a CHANGE

Lord, help me look beyond the walls of my classroom to strengthen families by...

Guard my own family by helping me to...

SCRIPTURES to Study
Commit it to MEMORY

"I have been reminded of your sincere faith, which first lived in your grandmother Lois and in your mother Eunice and, I am persuaded, now lives in you also."

—2 Timothy 1:5

■ Do you know the parents of the children you teach well enough to see a sincere faith in them?

■ Why would knowing Timothy's mother and grandmother be important for Paul (his teacher) to know?

Who Said THAT?

"While it is certainly true that children today are exposed to much more information than ever before, that exposure in and of itself does not guarantee that children will learn from the information if it is not talked about and examined."

—Dr. David Elkind,
Miseducation: Preschoolers at Risk

I Need a Vacation

Think It Over

Every ministry responsibility has big potential for burnout. Children's ministry is certainly no exception. However, burnout is not unavoidable. You can easily sidestep it if you understand what causes it and what you need to do to prevent it. If burnout were food, and 10 is "I'd be Uncle Herb's barbecued hamburgers" and 1 is "I'd be sushi," where are you on the burnout scale?

the ART of TEACHING

Your children's ministry probably has volunteers who have been teaching in children's ministry for ten, twenty, thirty, or even forty years. Your children's ministry probably has seen volunteers who didn't last a month. How do teachers keep going? What is the common denominator of teachers who remain in their ministry?

One of the most important attributes needed for every ministry position is the proper attitude. Do you have a sense of humor in the classroom? Do you focus on control and order or on learning and fun? If you are having a good time, children will have a good time. If you come into the classroom with a sense of dread, guess how children will respond to your lesson. Before you begin teaching, determine to come into the classroom with a good attitude that focuses on learning and fun. Good teachers teach because they love to teach. Teaching brings them strength and joy. They realize that the Christian walk is just as much about serving others as it is about personal growth in Christ.

Increase your love for teaching by not letting setbacks, hard work, or other disappointments drain you. Remember that every work of service presents obstacles and resistance. Difficulties are not an indicator of your success. Rather, your response to difficulties dictates your success. Have you had any good news lately in your area of ministry? Success breeds success. Create a reminder, build a monument, or make journal entries that will serve to remind you of how God has used you and why you are serving children!

Don't be afraid to take a timeout! When an athlete is exhausted, he or she can simply raise a hand to be taken off the field to rest up. The athlete will then return to the game with renewed energy and effectiveness. If you're sick when you're supposed to teach, find a substitute. If you need some time to get away and pray, take it! If your ministry provides natural breaks from teaching, use those times to recharge your batteries rather than look for another ministry or, worse yet, another church! ■

Flash in the Pan

William Shatner hosts a show that tells the story of rock bands that have had one major hit and then faded from the limelight. It is called *One Hit Wonders*. The stories of why these musicians were never heard from again are stories of burnout, boredom or bad behavior. While we may fully remember their songs, we have no clue about who they were or what they ended up doing. Such is the tragedy of what William Shakespeare calls a "bubble reputation"—here today and gone tomorrow.

SCRIPTURES to Study
* Commit it to MEMORY

"But the seventh day is a Sabbath to the Lord your God. On it you shall not do any work."

—Deuteronomy 5:14a

■ Why did God have to rest?

■ What should you do when you are at rest? What should you not do?

Take It Home

Often we think of vacations as large events that can only take place once or twice a year. But many people find joy in resting by taking one of the following mini-vacations or breaks. Choose to do one of these this week:

■ Spend the day at a prayer retreat center.

■ Get a foot massage at your local beauty center.

■ Take a walk around a lake, or if it is snowing, inside a mall.

■ Go out on a date.

■ Go to the library and read your favorite magazines or newspapers.

■ Don't eat lunch at your desk; eat it outside.

■ Wake up half an hour earlier and read one chapter in Psalms.

■ Play a board game as a family tonight after dinner (with the TV off).

It's time for a CHANGE

Lord, help me to slow down so I don't stop. Help me to pace myself by...

Who Said THAT?

"If you keep a bow always bent, it will break eventually; but if you let it go slack, it will be more fit for use when you want it."

—Aesop

Midseason Checkup

Think It Over

BUT IT'S ONLY HALFTIME!

Ecclesiastes 7:8 says, "The end of a matter is better than its beginning." Is your classroom building and strengthening for a great ending, or are you holding on only to fizzle out at the end of the year?

the ART of TEACHING

Remember those first few jobs you got paid for as a teenager? Do you remember how the time just lagged, the clock literally had battery issues, and the sun probably stood still? As you get older, you find that the seasons change at an alarming rate and time goes by too fast. As you review the first part of your teaching year, have you noticed that the weeks have been dragging like you're a teenager at work or flying by like you're a parent watching his or her children grow?

Halftime is fun if you're *winning* the game. "It's halftime already!" the team that is winning says. If you feel like a winning team, your primary task is to finish well. Rather than maintaining, keep improving. Look for ways to make your class even more fun and your teaching even more effective. Teams that sit on their lead during the second half often lose the game.

Halftime is another story if you're losing the game! It can be cruel, depressing, and disheartening. At halftime, teams either give up hope and give in or they refocus, adjust their game plan, and start the second half with renewed hope and determination. At halftime, a pep talk is usually not enough to bring about victory. If you feel like you're losing, you need to change your game plan.

Begin the change by praying and asking God for strength and direction. Ask your leader or fellow teachers for some help and advice on midcourse corrections, and look for ways to renew your energy as well as the energy of your students. You may find that you need a sweeping change such as combining your class with another to gain strength in numbers or you need to recruit another helper to support you during your lessons.

You may find that you need to make incremental changes that build to a rousing and jubilant finish to a great year of teaching. For example, you might give one portion of your next lessons to a group of sixth-graders as a special project. If this method succeeds, provide opportunities for more of your children to create, explore, and even teach. Rather than throwing out your entire format or lesson plan, you could commit to bringing in one truly creative activity to your class every week. If the children aren't having fun, the teacher is probably not having fun. Look for ways to make your lessons fun for the kids and let the momentum build. Whatever you do, don't give up! The difference between a dismal second half and a victory party may be only a few adjustments away. ■

No Failing, Just Learning

There is no greater failure than not learning from your mistakes. One man stands as an example of persistence and perseverance unlike any other. He failed in business in 1832. He was defeated for legislature in 1832. He failed again in business in 1833. He suffered depression in 1836. He was defeated for speaker in 1838. He lost his bid for Congress in 1843 and lost his run for Senate in 1855. He was defeated for vice president in 1856 and lost another run for the Senate in 1859. Finally, he was elected president in 1860. Some people, like Abraham Lincoln, have all the luck.

Take It Home

Like most worthwhile endeavors, teaching is hard work. There is no instant success (unless it is Cup-a-Soup). Sometimes taking that extra measure of attention will help you achieve extraordinary results. Try the following experiment. Get a large rubber band, and see how far you can shoot it. Mark the spot where you shot, and then stand back and shoot it again, each time trying to outshoot the first marker. Then ask yourself what made you hesitate to go further each time? How is that like or unlike the fear of failure in some people who want to quit? What fear do you have that may cause you to lose heart and slow down in your diligence in teaching?

It's time for a CHANGE

Lord, you are my strength and my future. Help me during this next season to...

SCRIPTURES *to Study*
* Commit it to MEMORY

"For this reason I remind you to fan into flame the gift of God, which is in you through the laying on of my hands. For God did not give us a spirit of timidity, but a spirit of power, of love and of self-discipline."

—2 Timothy 1:6-7

■ How would power, love, and self-discipline help you finish well?

■ How are your embers? Are they blazing, smoldering, or cold?

Who Said THAT?

"Perseverance is the hard work you do after you get tired of doing the hard work you already did."

—Newt Gingrich

Kid-to-Kid Connections

Think It Over

Hey! Is this what you learn in your Sunday school?

Can your students count at least five friends among their classmates at church? Are you helping them find good friends who will help them grow?

the ART of TEACHING

The word *collaboration* has recently emerged as an important element of Christian education. It's not new! Collaboration has been a staple in business for many years. W. Edwards Deming used it extensively in Japan after World War II. Deming, a management professor, was instrumental in transforming Japanese business into a world leader in quality and performance. He used the approach called collaboration, or teamwork. Teamwork is effective in the classroom as well as in business.

Encouraging child-to-child collaboration has many benefits. When children collaborate, they reach out to others they may not know very well. We often schedule and "program" our children so much at church that they rarely are given a chance to connect with one another. Collaboration also empowers children to recognize an important "body" principle. It helps eliminate cliques and builds unity in your church. Allowing children to work together produces results, answers, and questions that would otherwise be lost if children had to learn alone or passively.

It's so easy to foster collaboration. Simply look for opportunities to group children in pairs, trios, and groups of four. Have groups work together to answer questions, create projects, or solve problems. Some churches enlist teenage or adult volunteers to help facilitate small-group time. You'll be amazed to find how collaboration eliminates many disruptions and discipline problems. Instead of kids talking out of turn with their "neighbor," they are encouraged to interact because it is part of your lesson!

Encouraging children to interact can also have many positive effects on the teacher. Collaboration will give you a break from speaking! Rest your voice a bit, and listen to children sharing with one another. Collaboration will also give you an opportunity to prepare for the next activity. It will help you determine the intimacy level of your group. Most important, you can use that time to determine if your teaching is really connecting with kids!■

Work With Me

Benjamin Franklin was turned off to church as a boy growing up in Boston. By the time he became a young man in his new home of Philadelphia, he counted as his friend one of the greatest revivalists in England and America, George Whitefield. "I happened soon after to attend one of his sermons, in the course of which I perceived he intended to finish with a collection, and I silently resolved he should get nothing from me. I had in my pocket a handful of copper money, three or four silver dollars, and five pistoles in gold. As he proceeded I began to soften, and concluded to give the coppers. Another stroke of his oratory made me ashamed of that, and determined me to give the silver; and he finished so admirably that I emptied my pocket wholly into the collector's dish, gold and all."

SCRIPTURES to Study
Commit it to MEMORY

"But if we walk in the light, as he is in the light, we have fellowship with one another, and the blood of Jesus, his Son, purifies us from all sin."

—1 John 1:7

- What does fellowship look like in your classroom?

- Why do you think John equates walking with Jesus in the light to fellowship with one another?

Take It Home

Collaboration is the key to getting things done, but it is also a pain in the neck for some people who would rather do things themselves. Sometimes it's simply quicker to accomplish something alone! But does going solo contribute to a successful learning environment? Try this at home:

Have one or two people help you in a task you normally complete alone. For example, you might set the table, cook, or clean up together. Don't delegate the activity; have the person do it with you. Then think over the following questions:

- How did the interaction improve or deteriorate as you went along?

- What would you do differently next time?

- What does this experience teach you about collaborative learning?

It's time for a CHANGE

Lord, create a bond among my students by...

Who Said THAT?

"An ounce of encouragement after a failure [is] worth more than a pound of praise after a success."

—Dr. Marvin Marshall

Creative Crafts

Mom, is this anyone we know in our family?

Think It Over

God is the Master Creator. As beings made in God's image, we also have an appreciation for and desire to be creative. What benefits (beyond keeping children occupied) do you see in having children make crafts?

the ART of TEACHING

Many of us are not able to visualize a Popsicle stick turning into anything other than a tongue depressor. For some of us, crafts are just too messy. The thought of glue and glitter all over everything is enough to make us never attempt a project. Others just don't see the benefit of wasting valuable class time on this "busy work." Many teachers are very happy to go through an entire school year without ever venturing into a supply cabinet.

However, there are some children who really need to be creative. They need to explore, interpret, and understand the Bible story by creating a visual representation. They need the self-esteem that comes in saying, "Look what I made all by myself!" As a teacher, your task is not to develop lessons that are fun and comfortable for you. Rather, your task is to develop lessons that help children engage and learn.

The good news is that crafts have come a long way from the Popsicle stick crafts with which many of us grew up. There are many resources out there that have very simple, clear directions using minimal supplies. Also, any good craft book will have tie-ins to the lesson you are presenting. Crafts should never be just time-fillers. To be most effective, crafts always need to help reinforce your lesson. Making a jar full of bath salts may be nice and fun by itself. But the same craft has much more impact and value when you use it to teach children about sharing and caring. When you challenge children to give the craft away to someone in need, you have given them an experience they'll never forget.

One of the great outcomes of a craft project is that you can really see the unique creativity that God has put in everyone. Whenever possible, choose crafts that give the children the freedom to express themselves. All crafts should rarely look the same. If we want uniformity, we may as well pass out coloring books and make children color in the lines with all the same crayons. Sometimes the process of the project is as important as the product. When children are having a good time doing the project, they will enjoy the finished product even more. This will help them in retaining the lesson as well as help them think of your church and God in a positive light. ■

Take It Home

Sometimes we forget how a project can be so thrilling to experience for the first time. Try this at home.

Take a piece of paper and spread glue over most of it. Try using your fingers to spread the glue, and feel the sensation of it. Sprinkle a thick layer of salt all over the glue. Let it dry thoroughly. When the glue is dry, drop some watered-down food coloring on the salt.

Drop several colors close to each other. If you have a spray bottle, mist some water on the picture. How is this like spreading God's love? Be honest, wasn't the project fun? Imagine what a project could add to your classroom.

The Artistic Mind

The famous artist Picasso always forbade anyone to clean his studios or dust them. Picasso always counted on the layer of protection that dust gives. If he would see dust missing, he always knew someone had touched his things, and it bothered him. He also preferred to wear gray suits because it was the only color on which his dust would leave no trace.

SCRIPTURES to Study
* Commit it to MEMORY

"Where the Spirit of the Lord is, there is freedom."
—2 Corinthians 3:17b

- Do you hinder or encourage freedom to create in your classroom?

- How does freedom reflect the Spirit of the Lord?

It's time for a CHANGE

God is showing me that I need to be aware of the creative needs of my children. I may need to think more about...

Who Said THAT?

"Every child is an artist. The problem is how to remain an artist once he grows up."

—Pablo Picasso

Out-of-the-Box Training

Some days I feel I am losing it.

Think It Over

We live in an unprecedented age of accessible information for insight, knowledge, resources, and advice. Did you know that a majority of the training you can receive is a short drive from your front door? Get ready for a road map for training outside of the box!

the ART of TEACHING

The late Christian educator Frank E. Gaebelein said, "All truth is of God." That is, accurate principles, whether in Scripture or in the world of ideas or nature, are applicable when they are true! Whether we find helpful teacher training in the Word of God itself or in a parenting seminar at a local elementary school, truth belongs to God. Finding and applying that truth can be a fruitful and rewarding exercise. Where can you look in addition to Scripture, the church, or religious training to find teaching excellence?

Your local private school or public school district most likely has numerous resources to help teachers and parents enhance their understanding of how children grow and learn. Perhaps your school district offers newsletters or courses that would be helpful. Your community center may offer classes on parenting or learning. You can also volunteer to assist with coaching or teaching to learn more about children and how others teach them. The Internet also provides an almost overwhelming amount of information. For example, a Google search using the words *Attention Deficit Disorder* yields hundreds of thousands of results. When using the Internet, it's best to look for Web sites from established organizations with which you're familiar, as they have higher accountability for what they post. While it takes a little more effort to check out books from your library, you'll find that the information is usually more reliable in a published book.

Another great opportunity for learning is found in local field trips. Check out toy stores that have an educational bent to see what toy companies believe children find interesting. Visit play places, classrooms, or other areas where children gather. You may want to check in with the staff of the facility so your intentions are clear. Make a note of how children interact and what they find interesting. Then think about how that applies to your classroom. Your local community college or university often has continuing education courses or adult education evening classes for early childhood and elementary teachers. These classes can put you on the cutting edge without doing too much damage to your pocketbook. By using resources that are secular in focus yet biblical in application, you can become a fully informed, highly curious, and broadly educated teacher! Happy learning! ■

Keep Learning

College education is not just for high school graduates anymore. Lifelong learning is transforming the population at colleges and universities in the United States. According to Constantine Papadakis, the president of Drexel University, in the year 2000 there were

■ 3,900,000 undergraduates,

■ 700,000 graduates,

■ 2,900,000 semi-traditional full-time undergraduates,

■ 500,000 semi-traditional graduates, and

■ 5,500,000 non-traditional full-time undergraduates.

SCRIPTURES to Study
* Commit it to MEMORY

"Not that I have already obtained all this, or have already been made perfect, but I press on to take hold of that for which Christ Jesus took hold of me. Brothers, I do not consider myself yet to have taken hold of it. But one thing I do: Forgetting what is behind and straining toward what is ahead, I press on toward the goal to win the prize for which God has called me heavenward in Christ Jesus."

—Philippians 3:12-14

■ What helps you press on in your desire to grow?

■ How would forgetting what is behind you help you grow?

Take It Home

In the course of this week, take a moment to gather some insight, instruction, and innovative ideas from one of the following sources. Interview one teacher at a church that you've heard good things about. Browse a local Christian bookstore, and look at all the supplemental material for your classroom. Stop off at your local public library, and listen in on the children's story time to gather insight into story-telling techniques. Call the local elementary school or day-care center to see what courses they offer that you could take to enhance your own teaching skills.

TIC... TOC... TIC...

It's time for a CHANGE

Open my mind, Lord, as I press on to learn by putting off...

and putting on...

Who Said THAT?

"The illiterate of the 21st century will not be those who cannot read and write, but those who cannot learn, unlearn, and relearn."

—Alvin Toffler

The Balancing Act

I was wondering if you could cover for me tomorrow. I forgot that I was going to be on vacation and won't be able to teach!

Think It Over

There are two unhealthy extremes Christians often fall into when it comes to service and ministry. On one extreme, we neglect our call to reach out and serve by hiding behind our schedules or our families. On the other extreme, we neglect our families and health by serving beyond our capacity. Into which extreme do you tend to fall?

the ART of TEACHING

Life is like a teeter-totter: The game is only fun if the people on both sides assist one another and have similar weight distribution. If one child is heavier than the other, the smaller one dangles in midair. The goal is not balance but the equal distribution of weight to jump up and down! Likewise, in life our goal is not to give equal weight to God's work and our family responsibility. Rather, the goal is to place emphasis on the right one at the proper time with the appropriate energy.

Rather than asking, "What will I have to neglect today?" we should ask, "How will I make my role as a parent and my role in ministry successful today with the time I have available?" Both require commitment, and both are important to God's work in your life. You should be committed to seeing both areas of your life succeed. But you must be realistic about what you can and should do in both areas.

It's easy to avoid your call to focus on your family when things at home are unraveling. Ministry can become an escape. Busyness outside your home can delay or even deny the hard work required for a healthy home. Likewise, poor commitment to or performance in ministry can easily be excused with the demands that have been placed on you at home. Self-discipline is critical to striking a balance. Families understand that they will often be called upon to be flexible (especially during VBS week), just as churches are called upon to adjust to your home emergencies (such as a death in the family).

It's important to let your family and friends into your ministry. Having a spouse or friend who supports you is a powerful force in helping you reach your potential. Letting others into your ministry does not include gossip or griping. Both of those methods of letting off steam have nothing but negative effects on the speaker and the listener. Have your family and friends help you with your teaching responsibilities. Enlist their help in overcoming barriers, sharing successes, or just teaming up with you to serve! This collaboration will make your sacrifice a team effort, and your family will begin to understand the "why" behind your own service.

The discipline of balance is often found in adaptability. If you know you are coming into a particularly stressful time at home, work early on your lesson for next Sunday. If your spouse wants to take you away on a three-day weekend, find your own substitute for your class! If the work at church is frustrating, draining, and causing you to lose sleep, share your feelings with your spouse or friends; and ask them to pray with you for energy, creativity, and stamina. ∎

Industry

The late eighteenth century was a busy time in the new United States of America. The demands on the signers of the Declaration of Independence required extraordinary sacrifice. One family's secret to enduring so much depravation was to write letters, as John and Abigail Adams of Quincy, Massachusetts, did. They would typically send two or three letters a week. In one letter, Abigail complained, "No man even if he is sixty years of age ought to have more than three months at a time from his family." John Adams responded, "How dare you hint or list a word about 'sixty years of age'...I would soon convince you that I am not above forty."

SCRIPTURES to Study
Commit it to MEMORY

"You will keep in perfect peace him whose mind is steadfast, because he trusts in you."

—Isaiah 26:3

- Which priorities give you perfect peace?

- What does perfect peace feel like?

Take It Home

The old adage "Everything's OK, as long as everything's OK" is never more apparent than when our home relationships and church responsibilities are in alignment. This week call or visit an auto-repair shop that performs wheel alignment and balance. Ask the question "What are some of the problems that would happen to my car if I don't have the wheels balanced?" Then ask the question "What are some of the problems my car would have if I didn't have my wheels aligned?" How is alignment and balance important in your life?

It's time for a CHANGE

Lord, this week I am out of balance in this area of my life...

Who Said THAT?

"True balance requires assigning realistic performance expectations to each of our roles. True balance requires us to acknowledge that our performance in some areas is more important than in others. True balance demands that we determine what accomplishments give us honest satisfaction as well as what failures cause us intolerable grief."

—Melinda M. Marshall

Tell Me How I'm Doing

Think It Over

Do you look forward to your annual reviews? Unfortunately, evaluation is often incomplete, sometimes inaccurate, and often painful. However, evaluation is unavoidable if you want to grow. Do you welcome evaluation as a part of your growth, or do you work to avoid and rebuff it?

the ART of TEACHING

Peer review is a fundamental aspect of every teacher's training. It is an essential part of joining a team and playing by the same rules. Each teacher is part of a larger system that works to build and shape faith in children as they grow from toddlers to adults.

Review and input from other teachers allows the growing teacher to improve, adapt, and move toward excellence. While evaluation can be uncomfortable, teachers who want to be effective need to embrace it and even seek it out. With continued exposure to evaluation and basic guidelines for your reviews, you'll find that your peer reviews can become positive experiences that foster great discussion and brainstorming.

Before you begin, create a clear list of agreed-upon criteria upon which you will evaluate and be evaluated. One church looking for feedback for its children's ministry placed a questionnaire on its Web site that "looked back" (what had they done), "looked in" (how are they doing), and "looked ahead" (what they could do better). Whether a peer, a coach, or a customer (such as a parent or student) completes the evaluation, the criteria by which you are measured should be clear to both you and the parents of the children you teach.

When you were selected to teach, you were chosen because of your strengths. The evaluator or coach must work to point out how your strengths have a positive affect on the classroom. A review should serve to build up a teacher as much as it helps the teacher to make adjustments and improve. Evaluations are much more effective in the context of genuine relationship. Peers who don't know you will only offer general platitudes or highlight recently observed growth areas. Relationship allows the evaluator to work through difficult issues as well as offer genuine insight and praise.

Your church may have a formal evaluation process. However, your growth is your responsibility. Have the courage to grow. Ask another teacher to come in one Sunday and spend time with you. Ask a parent to come in and help point out something that could help you connect better with his or her child. Talk to your pastor or children's ministry leader over coffee or during dinner at your home and ask, "What can I do better?" ∎

Everyone's a Critic

The dedication of the cemetery at the Gettysburg battlefield was a somber occasion. The most memorable speaker of the day was the main speaker of the day, Edward Everett, the famous Massachusetts orator. His comments lasted more than two hours and were delivered from memory. At his conclusion, even Abraham Lincoln was impressed and said, "I am more than gratified, I am grateful to you." The original manuscript of Everett's speech is housed in the files at the Lincoln Presidential Library and Museum (www.alincoln-library.com). Lincoln's short speech began, "Fourscore and seven years ago." Afterward, Lincoln told an aide, "That speech won't *scour*," referring to the plows that failed in the prairie. But history was kinder, and the 269-word "short speech" by Lincoln is carved in granite at his memorial in Washington, D.C., and in the history books as one of the greatest speeches of all time. Beware the too hasty critique!

Take It Home

We often overlook areas in our lives that need to be improved, or we shyly become embarrassed when others point out our strengths. To understand your natural response to evaluation, place a "+" next to the areas listed below in which you welcome evaluation and feedback. Place a "-" beside those areas in which you'd rather not receive feedback. What do your marks say about your willingness to grow?

- Evaluation of your teeth from the dentist
- Evaluation of your health from the doctor
- Evaluation of your hairstyle
- Evaluation of your wardrobe
- Evaluation of your physical fitness from the trainer
- Evaluation of your work from your boss
- Evaluation of your teaching from your ministry leader
- Evaluation of art or music you create
- Evaluation of your diet from a dietician

It's time for a CHANGE

Lord, teach me through the wisdom of others. Help me to open myself up to growth by...

SCRIPTURES to Study
Commit it to MEMORY

"My son, do not despise the Lord's discipline and do not resent his rebuke, because the Lord disciplines those he loves, as a father the son he delights in."

—Proverbs 3:11-12

- How is receiving criticism similar to receiving discipline?
- How do you think the Lord's delight in you would be a motivation to receive criticism?

Who Said THAT?

"For people who like that sort of thing, that is about the sort of a thing they would like."

—Abraham Lincoln, to a young poet who had asked him what he thought of his newly published poems

Child Safety in the Classroom

This is the best way I've found to protect your child during our active learning hour.

Think It Over

Emotional safety is a prerequisite for nurturing learning and understanding about God, but equally important is the physical safety of the children in your classroom. Is your classroom really safe? How do you know?

the ART of TEACHING

There was a time not too long ago when a church worker didn't have to worry about a lawsuit when they changed a diaper, led a child to the potty, or spent one-on-one time with a child. Times have changed. Nothing will tear a church apart faster than an accusation of inappropriate behavior with a child. Nothing is more tragic than the hard reality that many of the accusations are true. Christ admonished us to be wise as serpents and innocent as doves. This instruction describes the very posture and mind-set you need to help provide a safe and secure environment for children in your care.

You can be wise as serpents in several ways. Make certain you have a co-worker present with you as much as is humanly possible. The "two-adult rule" has really become an essential reality in children's ministry. The premise behind this rule is that no adult teacher or helper will ever be alone with a child or a group of children. Having two adults in the same classroom at all times dramatically reduces the probability of abuse. The practice also protects teachers from unsubstantiated accusations that a child could make against any of your actions.

Many churches also require background checks and applications for all volunteers and staff who work with minors. Some state agencies conduct free or inexpensive background checks for nonprofit organizations that provide child care or instruction. Some insurance companies require these safety measures as part of their discount insurance rates. Churches also should develop policies regarding interaction between staff and volunteers with minors. If your church implements these safeguards, rejoice that your leaders are striving to make working with children safe for teachers and safe for children. If your church has not yet implemented these safeguards, find out why. Look for ways to encourage and support the church staff in making your church a safe place for your teachers and your children.

If you suspect or witness abuse, it's essential that you report it to the director of your children's ministry, your pastor, or local law enforcement agencies. Check with your children's ministry leader for your church's procedures for reporting injuries or abuse. The worst possible reaction to inappropriate or illegal behavior is to cover it up or deny it. A case of abuse that is handled quickly and appropriately is a heart-wrenching setback for a ministry. A poorly handled or ignored case of abuse is an ugly disaster that will destroy many lives, relationships, and possibly the entire church.

You can be innocent as doves in several ways. Ask God to create in you a clean heart. Make sure you leave anger, frustration, fatigue, or even bitterness against any child securely where it belongs—far from the classroom and at the foot of the cross. Talk to your pastor or children's ministry leader about situations or practices that have potential for danger. Also, work to protect children against themselves! Sometimes a child wants to live dangerously or even bolt from your classroom. Don't be afraid to involve parents and your leaders if a child presents a hazard to himself or herself or to other children in your classroom.

Jesus told us to be wise and innocent—not paranoid. You don't have to be afraid to teach, and you needn't look at other teachers with suspicion. Rather, be aware and be honest. Set up guidelines and precautionary measures so you can spend class time focusing on the real reason you're there—teaching children to know and love God. ■

Big Mistakes

According to the National Center for Injury Prevention and Control, "unintentional injuries are the *leading cause of death* in the United States for people aged 1-34. Each year, more than 90,000 people die in the U.S. as a result of unintentional injuries. During an average year in the U.S., unintentional injuries account for nearly 31 million emergency room visits."

SCRIPTURES to Study
Commit it to MEMORY

"But if anyone causes one of these little ones who believe in me to sin, it would be better for him to have a large millstone hung around his neck and to be drowned in the depths of the sea."

—Matthew 18:6

■ What is Jesus' attitude about causing children harm?

■ How can you protect the children in your care?

Take It Home

Have you ever noticed how some people spend a lot of time preparing the room for people who are coming while others make it an afterthought? Put a check next to the places listed below that you feel are safe and comfortable. Put an X through the places that try to make you feel like they don't want you to stay too long!

■ a doctor's office waiting room

■ Grandma or Grandpa's house

■ your best friend's home

■ your office

■ the auto-repair shop waiting area

■ the post office

■ Starbucks

■ Barnes & Noble

It's time for a CHANGE

God, please give me eyes that spot danger before it is felt and prevent harm before it hurts by...

Who Said THAT?

"The hearts of small children are delicate organs."

—Carson McCullers

Stop Child Abuse

Recognizing Child Abuse

Think It Over

Did you know that

there are four forms of

child abuse? They are

sexual abuse, physical

abuse, emotional

abuse, and neglect. As

a teacher, you are in a

unique position to

help stop violence.

But do you know the

outward or inward

signs of abuse?

the ART of TEACHING

Healthy families make up healthy communities. However, some children are raised in environments in which abuse is common and frequently tragic. Knowing the physical and nonphysical signs of abuse and then knowing how to report them could give a child a second chance and give you confidence to intervene when necessary.

According to an article from www.kidsource.com, Dr. Daniel Laskin, editor of the Journal of Oral and Maxillofacial Surgery, offers a list of some physical signs of abuse that could raise your suspicions, including jaw fractures, facial bruises, bruised or swollen lips, loose teeth, lacerations of the tongue and lips caused by forced feeding, abrasions of the corners of the mouth from the use of a gag, evidence of hair pulling, and bruising and tearing of the membrane in the ear. Other signs include multiple, anatomically unrelated injuries that can't be explained by the parent; evidence of physical or emotional neglect; malnourishment or malnutrition; and scars from previous injuries or injuries in various stages of healing.

Some nonphysical signs of abuse include immaturity, poor impulse control, low tolerance of frustration, a tendency to establish inappropriately rigid behavioral standards, and a child's own perception that he or she is under considerable emotional stress.

If you suspect abuse, your role is not to investigate. Your role and responsibility is to report. The Child Protective Services in your state is the investigative agency required by law to ascertain whether or not a finding of abuse exists. They can be contacted directly, or you can dial 911. In either case, your confidentiality is safeguarded by state and federal law. Often, there are state requirements that may make you a mandated reporter that would make it a criminal offense for you *not* to report abuse. Some laws require that teachers report abuse, neglect, threats or indications of suicide, and runaways.

Find out what the reporting procedure is for your church and local government. Many churches have incident/injury report forms to keep a record of all incidents, injuries, and signs of injuries. When you're making a report, it's usually best to simply relay the facts of the incident. For example, it may be appropriate to report that "Sara had three orange-sized bruises on her left leg above her calf." It would be dangerous to report that "Sara had three huge bruises on her leg that her uncle probably gave her with a belt." Including your personal opinions and assumptions can open you and your church up to liability. Denominational headquarters are usually happy to provide their churches with resources and advice on recognizing and reporting abuse. ∎

It Must Stop

According to the Centers for Disease Control in Atlanta, "Child maltreatment includes physical abuse, neglect (physical, educational, emotional and/or medical), sexual abuse, emotional abuse...and other types of maltreatment...or threats to harm the child. Every year an estimated 826,000 children experience non-fatal child maltreatment."

Everyone who comes in contact with children should be aware that the signs of abuse are not always readily apparent. By keeping a constant vigil for the related indicators of abuse, caregivers will be better able to bring these secrets out of the dark.

SCRIPTURES to Study
Commit it to MEMORY

"For the Lamb at the center of the throne will be their shepherd; he will lead them to springs of living water. And God will wipe away every tear from their eyes."

—Revelation 7:17

■ What hope does this verse bring you?

■ How does God "wipe away every tear" from you?

Take It Home

Call your local Child Protective Services agency and get information regarding reporting requirements for *mandated reporters* and spotting the signs of abuse.

Call your church pastor or children's ministry leader to find out the lines of reporting any suspicions of abuse. Ask for information from the church's insurance agency or legal counsel with regard to your liability. Ask when the next all-church training for volunteers will cover abuse policies or if any are in writing.

Finally, pray for the millions of children worldwide who are physically, sexually, emotionally, and brutally exploited every day. Let God create in you the strength to create a safe place for children!

TIC... TOC... TIC...
It's time for a CHANGE

God, show me if I need to take action about...

Who Said THAT?

"Child abuse casts a shadow the length of a lifetime."

—Herbert Ward, Episcopal priest

Pay Attention!: ADD Update

Think It Over

Attention-Deficit/
Hyperactivity Disor-
der affects nearly 2
million children and
young people. Since 3
to 7 percent of
school-age children
have this disorder,
your classroom proba-
bly has one or more
children who need
special attention. Can
you give it to them?

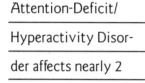

the ART of TEACHING

According to the 2000 American Psychiatric Association's *Diagnostic and Statistical Manual of Mental Disorders-IV*, Attention-Deficit/Hyperactivity Disorder is a disruptive behavior disorder characterized by ongoing inattention and/or hyperactivity-impulsivity occurring in several settings and more frequently and severely than is typical for individuals in the same stage of development. Symptoms often begin before children reach the age of seven. ADHD can cause serious difficulties in home, school, or work life. However, it can be managed through behavioral or medical interventions, or a combination of the two. While parents have oversight of medical interventions, the following are some helpful tips to enhance your behavioral skills in reaching these special children.

Avoid labeling or isolating children with special needs. Whenever possible, integrate them and encourage their participation as full members of the class. You will most likely need assistance from the parents in the form of advice based on past observations of success. It will also require a warm and accepting environment in which other children are free to ask questions and offer assistance.

Since ADD/ADHD often makes childhood friendships and peer relationships difficult, early intervention can help a child navigate his or her way into a proper peer role. Help children understand that friendships are important in their lives. Maintain an ongoing relationship with people who are important to this child, such as his or her parents. Encourage the child with ADD/ADHD to pair up with a buddy when possible. Mix up the groups until you find the right ingredient for success. You may find that the child excels when you pair him or her with an adult or teen helper during times of transition or other activities with which the child struggles.

Remember that children with ADD/ADHD often have complex problems that extend beyond simple behavior. They need love, acceptance, and assistance to succeed in the one hour you have to give them each week. Don't hesitate to ask for help if you can't do it alone. Don't neglect the unique contribution of every child in your classroom. And don't stop working to include every child in that same classroom. ■

At Risk

Children and adolescents with Attention-Deficit/Hyperactivity Disorder (ADHD) can have more frequent and severe injuries than peers without ADHD.

The Centers for Disease Control indicates that "children with ADHD are significantly more likely to be injured as pedestrians or while riding a bicycle, to receive head injuries, injure more than one part of the body, and be hospitalized for accidental poisoning. Children with ADHD may be admitted to intensive care units or have an injury result in disability more frequently than other children. Children with ADHD appear to have significantly higher medical costs than children without ADHD. Health care costs for each child with ADHD may be more than twice as high as medical costs for children without ADHD."

SCRIPTURES to Study
* Commit it to MEMORY

"A man with leprosy came to him and begged him on his knees, 'If you are willing, you can make me clean.' Filled with compassion, Jesus reached out his hand and touched the man. 'I am willing,' he said. 'Be clean!' "

—Mark 1:40-41

■ What filled Jesus with compassion?

■ What are some ways you can show compassion to children with ADD/ADHD?

Take It Home

To best understand what is going on in the mind of a child with ADD/ADHD, try this experiment when making a meal this week. Turn on the radio about as loud as a normal conversation to a station with which you are unfamiliar. Then start the vacuum cleaner and let it run. Next, open the cookbook to read the directions for dinner. Make sure the television is turned on and all the pets are in your kitchen while you prepare. Next, have as many family members as possible talk to you while you prepare.

Now stare out the window, and watch the neighborhood wonder just how you can do it every day with such a noisy home! This is the daily routine of a child who perceives simultaneously everything around him or her and is unable to discriminate or subjugate various sounds or sights.

It's time for a CHANGE

God, give me compassion, energy, and the skill necessary to love those who are tough to touch by...

Who Said THAT?

"Growing numbers of children are suffering needlessly because their emotional, behavioral, and developmental needs are not being met by those very institutions which were explicitly created to take care of them."

—Surgeon General David Satcher

Making Scripture Stick

Today I learned that the Bible is a lamp unto my feet and sharper than any two-edged sword... I like the sword the most.

Think It Over

When was the last time you memorized a verse from a new song? a new PIN number? When was the last time you memorized a phone number? When was the last time you memorized a co-worker's name or a customer's preferences? Now when was the last time you memorized a verse from Scripture?

the ART of TEACHING

The ancient practice of memorization was a matter of necessity. A very small portion of the population was able to read or write. Scrolls were so precious that they were stored in the synagogue or library. The original Ten Commandments were chiseled in stone and were certainly too heavy to be mass-produced. Tablets of clay and papyrus were so expensive in the ancient world that only the very wealthy could own them. Memory, then, was the first practice of people who wanted to learn. Times have changed, but for many teachers, memorizing facts and Scripture is still the main method of learning the Ten Commandments, knowing the fruit of the Spirit, or even finding the books of the Bible.

Why are we more likely to memorize phone numbers and names than to commit passages of Scripture to memory? The key motivation is how it is going to be used, isn't it? If you are going to use the information, then you are more inclined to endure the hard work in committing it to memory.

It's great to have children memorize Scripture. However, the memorized verse is so much more valuable if children understand what it means and how it applies to their lives. Three-year-old Moriah knew all the words to the song "I Am a C." After listening closely, the girl's dad realized that instead of spelling *Christian*, the little girl was crooning, "I am a sea. I am a sea witch. I am a sea witch esh tee I en." Moriah didn't know what it meant to esh tee I en, but she was familiar with sea witches from *The Little Mermaid*. Spelling the word *Christian* didn't have any value for Moriah (although she liked the tune), because letters didn't mean anything to her yet.

The key to Scripture memory in the classroom is to keep pace with how much the children can use! If you encumber a child with a volume of memory that far outpaces his or her ability to use or understand it, the child will store the Scriptures only in short-term memory rather than long-term life-changing practice! Scripture is shown to be powerful when it is understood and the principles are applied personally today. Since our culture is blessed with so many copies of the Bible, perhaps it would be more profitable to emphasize daily reading or really digging into one or two verses that have meaning for a child's life. ■

Its Own Reward

In order to get children to memorize, we often resort to prizes or gimmicks. In a famous experiment designed to assess extrinsic versus intrinsic motivation, the experimenters took a group of preschool children and divided them into three groups. One group was told to draw with a promise of a reward. Another group was told to draw with no expectation of a reward. The final group was given unexpected rewards. The researchers then assessed the amount of free time spent playing with the markers one week later to assess intrinsic motivation to draw.

The study found that children who had played for an expected reward showed less intrinsic motivation to play later compared to children who had played for no reward or who had received an unexpected reward. This is called the "over-justification effect," when a behavior is over-rewarded and is no longer viewed as intrinsically important.

Choose three verses to memorize this week. Don't pick easy ones or ones that you already know. Choose one of the following ways of memorizing each verse. Write the verse on an index card, and repeat it three times in the morning and three times in the evening. Make up a song with the verse as the lyrics. Spend some time praying the verse aloud to the Lord and asking God to help you follow what it commands, suggests, or helps you do.

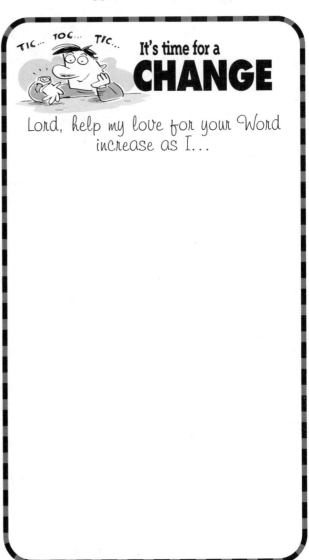

It's time for a CHANGE

Lord, help my love for your Word increase as I...

SCRIPTURES to Study
✱ Commit it to MEMORY

"I have hidden your word in my heart that I might not sin against you."

—Psalm 119:11

■ How does hiding God's Word in your heart help you not sin?

■ Besides memorizing, what are other ways to hide God's Word in your heart?

Who Said THAT?

"I am always ready to learn, although I do not always like being taught."

—Winston Churchill

 Published in *Teacher Training on the Go* by Group Publishing, Inc., P.O. Box 481, Loveland, CO 80539. www.grouppublishing.com

You Make a Difference

Think It Over

When your work is done, you've cleaned up the room, and you're driving home, do you ever wonder if you made an impact? Do all the people who have helped you grow in faith or inspired you know that they did?

the ART of TEACHING

Don't you love immediate feedback? Your cooking is right on when it is eaten with smiles and yummy moans. Your advice is correct when it is obeyed with dazzling results. Yet when it comes to determining if your classroom is filled with future Billy Grahams or Mother Teresas, the jury is still out.

But is it? The Barna Research Group has some interesting statistics that might shed some light on your promising progeny.

Barna has found that adults who regularly attended church as children were more likely than their unchurched peers to bring their own children to church (63 percent versus 33 percent). "Attending a church appears to be more a function of one's personal experience when young than a sense of responsibility to one's own children," explained George Barna. "There is no difference in the likelihood of attending a church these days among those who were churched as a child, regardless of whether they presently have children of their own or not."

The fact that children attend your class increases the statistical likelihood that generations to come will continue on in the faith. But your reach is much more important and powerful than statistics. Consider the following thoughts from a Sunday school teacher from Group Publishing's *Heartfelt Thanks for Sunday School Teachers*:

"I even remember some of my teachers' names—Mr. and Mrs. Applebee, for example. I remember them as being quite old even when they were my teachers, and I remember their many years of dedication in our church. Other teachers' names I can no longer recall.

"But if I could remember their names, I would try to contact them all to tell them that they're part of the reason I'm involved in ministry today. I can't remember my kindergarten teachers' faces, but I do remember how good it felt to help them make fancy folds in the take-home papers and pass them out after class. I remember how great it was to be chosen to help tell the Bible story by moving the characters in the sand table or the big, colorful, felt pieces during the story.

"As I got older, I valued having the freedom to ask a question about God if I wanted to. As an adult visiting a new church that was bigger than the one I grew up in, I responded immediately when a teacher came up to me right away, shook hands, introduced me to his wife, and invited me to join their small group...

"God knows the needs of the students who walk into your classroom each week. And God prepares your heart to touch their lives, whether you realize it or not."

Whether you realize it or not, you are making a tremendous difference. ∎

That's Some Nice Junk—

The Public Broadcasting Service's *Antiques Roadshow* features ordinary people lined up with their personal collectibles, antiques, and garage-sale-quality junk. They are waiting to have it appraised by experts. Much like the anticipation of a lottery drawing, folks can't wait to see how valuable their junk really is.

At the appraisal event in Tucson, Arizona, a man discovers that his rather plain-looking Navajo blanket is a "national treasure" and one for the *Roadshow* record books. Appraiser Don Ellis, of the Donald Ellis Gallery, is flabbergasted when the owner tells him he generally kept the blue-and-white blanket folded over the back of a chair. The appraiser describes it as an extremely rare piece from about 1840 to 1860, hand-woven and dyed to be worn by a Ute chief. Appraised at $350,000 to $500,000, the blanket is the most valuable item ever appraised on *Antiques Roadshow*.

How many of your children would be deemed treasures ten, twenty-five, or fifty years from now in God's ultimate roadshow?

SCRIPTURES *to Study*
Commit it to MEMORY

"Let us not become weary in doing good, for at the proper time we will reap a harvest if we do not give up."
—Galatians 6:9

■ What do you hope the children you teach will be like in twenty years?

■ How have you reaped a harvest in ministry?

Take It Home

Visit a nearby tree nursery, or walk around your yard this week and notice two types of trees: hardwood and softwood trees. Ask the nursery employee to tell you how quickly the softwood tree generally grows compared to the hardwood tree. Ask which type of tree is more valuable or more desirable for furniture and homes. How is that like or unlike what happens to the children in your own classroom?

TIC... TOC... TIC...
It's time for a CHANGE

Lord, when I feel like giving up, encourage me to remain steadfast by...

Who Said THAT?

"A diamond is a piece of coal that stuck to the job."

—Michael Larsen,
Literary Agents: What They Do, How They Do It, and How to Find and Work with the Right One for You

Care Beyond the Classroom

I'm not dressed for Sunday school until tomorrow!

Think It Over

Do you remember thinking that your teacher actually lived at school? What did you feel the first time you saw your school-teacher at the grocery store? When your children see you out-side the classroom, what do they imme-diately feel?

the ART of TEACHING

You can actually shape a student's life by what you do outside the walls of your classroom. If you're a veteran teacher, have you noticed the gaze of teenagers who had you when they were younger? Do you look out for students in your classroom after church in the halls and greet them by name? Your impact outside of the classroom is powerful. And the impact extends beyond the children to their friends and parents. According to Aberdeen Group research director Harry Watkins, a person shares a bad experience with an average of ten people, but they only share a good experience with two! Which means that you have to work five times as hard to have a positive impact.

One of the easiest and most effective ways to have a positive impact outside of the classroom is to remember the names of your children. Nothing communicates that you care about someone like calling him or her by name. Even people you don't know very well will talk like old friends when you greet them by name in a busy supermarket or a noisy restaurant.

Try your best to remember their special occasions. Do children in your class get birthday cards or e-mail notes on special days? You can't possibly remember every child's birthday, but you can write each birthday on your calendar and follow up. When a child tells you about an important event in his or her life, write it in your calendar so you can follow up with questions or a card. Every child matters to God. Since you are a spokesperson for God, let each child know how God feels about his or her life on special days!

Work to remember each child's special stories. Did a child share a prayer request in class or relay a particularly hurtful week to you? Write a note of encouragement or a postcard that lets the child know that his or her feelings matter to you! Follow up to see how God has answered the child's prayer or if you need to keep praying. A prayer log will remind you to follow up and can serve as a great tool to show how God has answered a child's prayers.

You can make a lifelong impression on a child by coming to the child's school to eat lunch, showing up for one of the child's recitals or sporting events, or inviting the family over for dinner. Showing care and concern out-side the classroom is not completely a function of the calendar or computer organizer! It is a matter of the heart. Spontaneity and whimsy will create an atmosphere that truly stands above the distractions and heartbreaks of a child's world. ■

She likes me after Sunday school too!

That's Follow-Up!

A Sunday school teacher in Arlington, Texas, told a remarkable story related to his routine of sending out an "I Missed You" note each week.

After nearly a year of sending out an "I Missed You" note to a particular child, Larry was beginning to wonder if there was any point to sending any more cards when he received a phone call from a woman. The caller was crying and nervous as she began, "I don't know anyone at our church, so I called you." This distraught mom decided to call the one person she knew at the church—her daughter's Sunday school teacher, whose postcards were delivered with regularity every week to their home. Her husband had just informed her that he was leaving, and she needed help.

"I didn't know what to say to her. Heck, I was just a fifth-grade Sunday school teacher," said Larry. But this teacher knew who could help. He told the mom that he would get back to her in a few minutes but that he needed to call one of the pastors at the church. "One of our pastors met with this family, and their marriage was saved." Even he was surprised at the long-term effect of a simple postcard sent faithfully to an absent student.

SCRIPTURES to Study
*Commit it to MEMORY

"By this all men will know that you are my disciples, if you love one another."

—John 13:35

■ In what ways does loving others show you are a disciple or follower of Christ?

■ How have you been showing love?

Take It Home

Who was the last person you sent a card to? In an age of e-mails and instant messages, it is the handwritten note that counts. Your assignment this week is to pick up that pen, go buy those cool stamps that aren't in a roll of a hundred, and start naming the things you appreciate in your children! For extra credit, mail them so they arrive on Saturday before your class time!

It's time for a CHANGE

Lord, free me from the tyranny of the urgent to spend time this week...

"It is only our deeds that reveal who we are."

—Carl G. Jung,
The Development of Personality

The Place of Play in Learning

Think It Over

I am so proud of Kevin. Look how he is re-enacting the building of Jericho. He is using his large motor skills by stacking the blocks while he is using his cognitive skills in looking for the right sizes to fit together. His interpersonal skills are increasing as he interacts with his friends. I am sure he will remember this story for a long time.

Why do they just play in this class? I wish they would learn something.

Imagine washing dishes in your kitchen sink. Do you think of this job as work or play? Imagine a young child washing dishes in your sink with a washcloth and a squirt bottle of soap. How does a child view that activity? Many activities are seen as play in a child's eyes because new activities bring new challenges. How can play be an important part of learning?

the ART of TEACHING

Many people who work with young children can see that learning takes place as they play. The more we learn from research, the more we learn that play is not something we merely do *instead* of learning. Play is how children normally experience their world. Children take what they know and expand on it. Without the ability to manipulate their environment through play, learning is inhibited.

By creating classrooms void of play, we actually create classrooms that limit learning. This, of course, is *not* an excuse to come to class without objectives, directions, or preparation. Learning through play must be organized and intentional. Teachers need to set up interest centers that allow creative expression while they direct probable outcome of the learning. By giving children general goals and guidelines for play, teachers can make sure that children apply and explore the content of the lesson. Learning is enhanced and strengthened through careful preparation.

Once you have set up an environment in which a child can explore and "try on" a Bible truth, expect questions. Parents will often question motives behind what looks like silly play. Help parents, teachers, and leaders who are more comfortable with traditional methods of learning understand your goals and rationale. Assure others that your goal is to teach the Bible story in a way that will make it more memorable for children. And making the Bible memorable should be one of the primary goals of any teacher or parent. If joyful play will help the process, then bring on the playtime! ■

Make a game out of an ordinary chore you or your family members have to complete often. For example, you could see who can build the highest tower out of clean silverware and then race to take down the tower and put the silverware away. As you develop your game, think about what elements must be present for the game to be fun. Can you have fun and still accomplish the task at the same time? What does it take to make Bible learning fun for children?

Let's Relax

Psychologist David Elkind has done extensive research into what happens to children who are not allowed to play. He maintains that many parents now "over-program" their children by enrolling them in too many activities. Consequently, all of their time is programmed and they have no opportunities to play freely. The result, according to Elkind, is that more children are suffering from stress, emotional and mental breakdowns, and other conditions that used to be considered adult diseases and conditions.

It's time for a CHANGE

We can be tempted to use our adult words and adult ways as we communicate with children. I can resist this temptation and play more like a child by...

SCRIPTURES to Study

Commit it to MEMORY

"And whoever welcomes a little child like this in my name welcomes me."

—Matthew 18:5

■ What kinds of activities would welcome a child into a room?

■ Why are laughter and fun important elements in the classroom?

Who Said THAT?

"The point is to develop the childlike inclination for play."

—Albert Einstein

Keeping Current

Think It Over

Does the music on the popular radio station drive you nuts? Do you recognize the characters on the shirts of the children in your class? Do you know which cartoons are great for learning and which ones are trash? Have you kept current with the children in your classroom, or have they left you in the dust?

the ART of TEACHING

In order to bring the Scriptures to life, you must know two very important worlds: You must be a student of the world of Scripture and a curious interpreter of the world of children. You have the wonderful opportunity to create in the life of a child a connection to the ancient and enduring truths of Scripture. Failure to understand the culture of children can result in irrelevance or irreverence. Let's become missionaries and try to adapt our message (that never changes) to the culture (which constantly changes).

A child's cultural world can be divided into a few general categories: There are the values that children pick up from the adults and peers around them; the music styles that often demonstrate a particular socioeconomic or identity group; and the dress and talk associated with children that distinguish them in the culture they have chosen or received.

How can you best understand a child's life in these distinct categories? Become a student of a child's friends. Do you hear what they are talking about, what they care about, and how they interact? Listen to a child's music and media choices. Knowing what children are being fed will help you understand how they are growing. Don't be afraid to expose yourself to the culture of children while keeping a distinction between your world and a child's world. Finally, become all things to all people so that you can by all possible means reach them with the truths of Scripture.

Remember that our message is unchanging, and the world of children is constantly in flux. Teachers should not change the message or pretend to be someone they're not. Rather, we must adapt our methods to speak the language of children's lives or else we will fail to help children connect with the most important lessons they can ever learn. ■

Tourists, Go Home

It has been variously referred to as manners, etiquette, and protocol. How one acts in a particular social situation demonstrates either a snobbish ignorance or a humble and submissive guest. Consider these cultural standards from various countries for something as simple as the concept of time.

In the United States we often say, "Time is money," and even Nike says, "Just do it!"

"He who rushes, arrives first at the grave."—Spanish proverb

"Haste is the devil's work and patience is from the Merciful."—Arabic proverb

"The peanuts don't grow until the rains come."—Zaire proverb

"If you wait long enough, even an egg will walk (the chicken will hatch)." —Ethiopian proverb

SCRIPTURES to Study
Commit it to MEMORY

"He was in the world, and though the world was made through him, the world did not recognize him."

—John 1:10

■ How did Jesus get to know us?

■ When has someone missed your efforts to reach him or her with God's love?

Take It Home

Visit a large toy store like Toys "R" Us or Zany Brainy. Ask a sales associate to point you to the most popular toys for children of the age level you teach. Do you find anything troubling about the toys to which you were pointed? What do the toys say about the world of children? How can you use one of the toys to teach children about God's Word?

TIC... TOC... TIC...

It's time for a CHANGE

Lord, please help me to connect the world of Scripture with the world of children by...

Who Said THAT?

"Children are great observers but lousy interpreters."

—Dr. Scottie May, Asst. Professor of Educational Ministries, Wheaton College, Wheaton, IL

Food Fun

Think It Over

the **ART** of **TEACHING**

Snack time does not have to be an unrelated interruption in your class. What if you could feed the body and soul at the same time? Graham crackers can be eaten as children stare in silence. Or children can make the crackers into a tent to help illustrate the wandering of the children of Israel in the Sinai Peninsula—with a little help from some frosting "glue"!

Everyone loves food! If you regularly serve a snack in your class, one of the first questions you probably hear every week is "When can we have our snack?" If you're going to feed children anyway, why not use food to feed their spirits as well as their bellies? Food is a great tool to add to your storytelling repertoire. The more senses you can engage in a lesson, the more memorable it will be.

Christian bookstores offer books that are entirely devoted to edible Bible crafts. Many of the books offer entire devotions built around food fun. You may create an entire ark out of vegetables and cantaloupe or have children make stones in the Jordan River with cream cheese, celery, and raisins. You can use food items to help you tell the story. For instance, when Jonah is tossed into the sea, you could give out Goldfish crackers. If you don't have time to pull together a creative devotion with food, you can use any snack to teach children about serving. Have children take turns preparing, serving, and cleaning up.

No matter how you present the snack, remember some important precautions: Always have people who handle food wash their hands before beginning. Use wet wipes or bacterial gel at the very minimum. You must also always be aware of food allergies in your classroom. The most common problems are found in peanuts, milk, and dyes. Peanut butter is one of the world's best edible cements. However, some allergies are so severe that mere peanut fumes can cause reactions. When a child joins your class, have parents fill out a card that includes medical information and allergies. Make sure all the teachers in your classroom understand the severity of the allergies. Be careful to never serve foods that pose a choking hazard to young children. Hotdogs, grapes, and hard vegetables can be lethal to children who aren't experienced chewers.

With some precautions in mind, there is no end to how food can be utilized in the storytelling process. Children may still ask you about snack time, but you can now look forward to it as an essential component of your lesson. Rather than a time-filler or a means to tide children over, snack time will help children know, love, and follow God.

Bon appétit! ■

Take It Home

Make a meal with your family or friends. The best way to get everyone involved is to make a pizza. As you are working, read Exodus 16:13-36. Ask your family or friends the following questions:

■ Why do you think it was important to put manna in the Ark of the Covenant?

■ What do you think the people felt about God after that first morning?

■ What other stories in the Bible revolve around food, and what does that say about God's love?

Foodtastic!

The pygmy shrew is known to eat up to its own weight every day. Deprived of nutrition for a day, it may starve to death. (Aren't you glad you aren't a shrew?)

Four tablespoons of ketchup, about the amount you would eat with an order of fries, contains the nutritional equivalent of an entire medium tomato. (Makes you feel better about those fries, doesn't it?)

Pumpkin seeds actually improve in nutritional value as they get older. (Too bad more foods in the backs of our refrigerators don't have this quality.)

It's time for a CHANGE

I want to use the sense of taste differently in the classroom by...

SCRIPTURES to Study
*Commit it to MEMORY

"Better a meal of vegetables where there is love than a fattened calf with hatred."

—Proverbs 15:17

■ What does this say about how we approach activities in our classroom?

■ What does this say about how intricate or complicated our teaching needs to be?

Who Said THAT?

"Some things you have to do every day. Eating seven apples on Saturday night instead of one a day just isn't going to get the job done."

—Jim Rohn

If you can't stand the sheep, get out of the pasture·ate.

Making the Most of Interruptions

Think It Over

Our character is more quickly revealed in our response to circumstances than by the programs we prepare. How prepared are you for the unplanned?

the ART of TEACHING

Thinly disguised as teachable moments are those interruptions that can knock the slats out from under us. These moments are thinly disguised because they are not what we obviously planned for; we planned for our *lesson*! They are teachable moments because they are the moments our students are most alert to what we have to say next!

A group of irate parents decides to give you a piece of their mind that they cannot afford to lose...in front of you and your kids. A child interrupts a puppet show by running up and hugging the puppet. Spills, fights, whispering, bolting for the door, even the call of nature can seem like interruptions to your well-planned lesson. But how can you turn these inevitable flow-stoppers into showstoppers?

Remember, often our first response is our worst response! If you pause, take a deep breath, get a grip on your emotions, even smile and look wide-eyed as you plumb your mind for a what-to-do-next strategy, you'll buy some valuable time! That time will help you come up with an appropriate response.

The best response redirects and refocuses the classroom toward your goal for that morning. The appropriate response varies according to the incident. For spills, for instance, a good strategy to redirect might be to use humor: "Oh, no, Mr. Apple Juice! What are you doing out of your cup? Let's get Mr. Brawny and clean you up!" This response would be better than blaming the child for carelessly spilling and focuses on a solution to the problem rather than its cause.

Finally, fight to maintain self-control. Self-control is a fruit of the Spirit. Unfortunately, it's not an inherited trait. God will give you the ability to be calm and in control even in the worst circumstances. Let your children observe the power of God to calm the storm of classroom interruptions by observing your self-controlled behavior. And when you do make a mistake, admit it! Apologize and move on.

My son's preschool teacher had a great phrase that my son learned one day when the teacher's classroom obviously got the best of her. Christopher came home and said, "Mrs. Murphy told us that she was 'zasperated' today!" Chris, who was only three at the time, knew how his teacher felt because she was honest and expressive about her frustration! "Tomorrow I'm not going to 'zasperate' her anymore!" was this little guy's response to what became a wonderful teachable moment. ■

It's time for a CHANGE

Lord, help me show myself prepared for whatever you send by...

A Little Too Prepared

According to the church records at Hartselle First Baptist Church, a visiting evangelist in about 1910 put a pistol on the pulpit and said, "I'm not finished with what I said and if any of you have anything to say about it, I'm ready." Everyone listened to what he had to say.

SCRIPTURES to Study
* Commit it to MEMORY

"Therefore do not worry about tomorrow, for tomorrow will worry about itself. Each day has enough trouble of its own."

—Matthew 6:34

■ How should we prepare for tomorrow if we should not worry about it?

■ What are you worrying about right now?

Take It Home

Planning for the unexpected is not something that we normally think of, but we should. Each day this week, take the following emergency test to see if you are prepared for the unexpected:

■ **Monday:** You're driving in the snow, and your car begins to fishtail. If you live in an ice-free climate, you are driving, and your car's brakes suddenly fail. What do you do first?

■ **Tuesday:** Your phone goes out at home, along with your electricity. What do you want to do first?

■ **Wednesday:** Who is the beneficiary in your life insurance policy? Who is the second beneficiary should the first pass away before you do?

■ **Thursday:** Do you have enough money or frequent flier miles saved to make an emergency airplane flight for a family funeral? Do you know whom to call if you do?

■ **Friday:** You are in another country when you lose your passport and all your cash. Who would you call, or where would you go first?

■ **Saturday:** You just cut some limbs off your largest tree when you accidentally cut a vein in your arm. You are all alone. What do you do first?

Who Said THAT?

"We cannot make it rain, but we can see to it that the rain falls on prepared soil."

—Henri J.M. Nouwen

Make It Open-Ended

What's brown, furry, has a long tail, collects nuts, and lives in trees?

I know the answer is "Jesus," but it sure sounds like a squirrel to me!

Think It Over

Students are not all alike. When you ask a question, some students fire back answers before you even finish. Other students need significant time to process the question and then formulate responses. How can you ask questions that allow all students to participate in your lesson?

the ART of TEACHING

Young children can't completely grasp abstract concepts. So adults inherently ask children close-ended questions that require concrete factual recall. The question "How was school today?" typically gets the short answer "Fine." But it doesn't take abstract reasoning ability for children to answer open-ended questions. You can ask the same question a different way: "What were your favorite parts of recess?" and follow it up with "Why do you enjoy doing those things?" Making room in your questions promotes thinking and helps you assess what really is going on in the minds of your students!

Open-ended questions are important in the classroom because not all students learn the same way. Some students get lulled into a sense of predictability when questions are always the same. "How many" this and "where was" that questions typically appeal to the few students with a penchant for minutiae. Many students are not as confident in a classroom. When you ask an open-ended question, when you care more about the process toward truth than finding the correct answer, children gain confidence. Children also invest time in processing and answering the question because they know every question is for every child.

You can ask open-ended questions by using some very well placed "hows" and "whys." Usually asking questions about feelings draws children into the discussion. For example, instead of asking, "How many stones did David pick up?" consider asking, "What do you think David thought or felt as he looked up and saw Goliath?" and "How would you feel?" Jerome Berryman, a professor of early childhood education, has urged teachers to use the term "I wonder" to invite a sense of imagination in a child that motivates learning and discovery. A close-ended question is predetermined and predictable. There is only one right answer, and the path toward reaching that answer is never analyzed. An open-ended question allows for a variety of responses and elicits very different thoughts. ■

Raising the Bar

In his biography *Surprised by Joy: The Shape of My Early Life*, C.S. Lewis relates the habits and essence of his favorite teacher. Smugy was Lewis' form master when Lewis was a young boy, and Lewis was struck by his "perfect courtesy."

Lewis wrote, "He always addressed us as 'gentlemen' and the possibility of behaving otherwise seemed thus to be ruled out...His manner was perfect: no familiarity, no hostility, no threadbare humor; mutual respect; decorum...Thus, even had he taught us nothing else, to be in Smewgy's form was to be in a measure ennobled. Amidst all the banal ambition and flashy splendors of school life he stood as a permanent reminder of things more gracious, more humane, larger and cooler."

Take It Home

Turn the following close-ended questions into open-ended questions. For example, "What is the third commandment?" could be changed to "When is it wrong to use God's name? Why is God's name so special?"

Now you try it with the following close-ended questions:

- Is the story of Jonah and the ark in the Old or New Testament? (Trick question.)

- What gifts did the Magi from the East give to baby Jesus?

- Who were the first to hear about the birth of Jesus?

- Where did Paul go in Damascus when he was blinded?

It's time for a CHANGE

Lord, open my heart that I might reflect again on the wonder of...

SCRIPTURES to Study
✳ Commit it to MEMORY

"What do you think about the Christ? Whose son is he?"
—Matthew 22:42a

- How could this open-ended question be answered by a Christian?

- How could this open-ended question be answered by a non-Christian?

Who Said THAT?

"Renunciation of thinking is a declaration of spiritual bankruptcy."

—Albert Schweitzer,
Out of My Life and Thought: An Autobiography

Rewards and Bribes

It's easy. She scoops up more than a pound of candy and then starts substracting some.

I always scoop up less than a pound and then add to it.

Think It Over

Fund-raising companies have proven that trinkets and small prizes go a long way in motivating children to work hard. Prizes and rewards motivate children, but do they offer the right motivation for learning God's Word?

the ART of TEACHING

There's no doubt that rewards and treats have power to motivate children. For a small reward, kids will learn memory verses, sit still, line up quickly, raise their hands, and even remain silent and attentive. However, results don't necessarily indicate success. Psychologists have noted for years that fear and guilt motivate children and accomplish desired results in outward action. While immediate results are achieved, the long-term negative effects of guilt and fear as motivators outweigh their value for temporary control. In addition, compliance is only pseudo-learning and is a dangerous substitute for critical thinking, Christian understanding, or even life change.

There are significant dangers that ministries must consider when trying to motivate children to learn using prizes or rewards. The primary danger is that the reward becomes the focus for the learner. When working for rewards, children can lose sight of the intrinsic value of knowing God's Word. Rather than finding motivation in God's love or their identity as God's children, kids concentrate on getting stuff. As children acquire stuff, the demand for more stuff becomes greater. The object being rewarded becomes less interesting and less desirable.

Think about your own work. You most likely receive a paycheck for the work you do. Is your paycheck motivating you everyday on the job? Or is the job you do a reward in itself? People work with both mind-sets. Which mind-set would you say is preferable? Do we want children to count on the prize rather than understanding the point, the goal, or the simple joy of learning? We really wouldn't need rewards if children were interested in the first place. It's easier to ask for compliance through a reward than to work hard to create a compellingly interesting story, classroom, or opening to our teaching time.

The alternative is clear. We need to create learning environments that motivate children intrinsically rather than motivate children extrinsically in the midst of a drab learning environment. Put a little spice back into the lesson by using material that is relevant, fun, interesting, and a little daring! Look to supplemental materials published by results-conscious companies. Get feedback from your students on how to motivate them. Make sure your ratios of leaders-to-children are small enough to create a climate in which learning is individualized, customized, and personal. Rewards may work, but are they really the best method for teaching children the truth of God's Word? ■

What's Your Motivation?

There are basically five explanations for how we are motivated. Instinct says our behavior is preprogrammed. Sociobiology says a genetic inheritance explains our behavior. Drive explains that our actions are motivated by an internal desire to seek balance from want or excess. Incentives are the main reason we seek pleasure and avoid pain. Finally Abraham Maslow showed that there is a hierarchy of needs. First our basic needs must be met for food and security and love before we can grow toward greater actions.

SCRIPTURES to Study
Commit it to MEMORY

"The goal of this command is love, which comes from a pure heart and a good conscience and a sincere faith. Some have wandered away from these and turned to meaningless talk. They want to be teachers of the law, but they do not know what they are talking about or what they so confidently affirm."

—1 Timothy 1:5-7

■ What motivates your love for children?

■ How would having a noble goal help you motivate students to learn?

Take It Home

Make a list of all the things you do because you want to—for example, you might include items like teaching children or going to church. Now make a list of all the things you do because of what you get—for example, you might include items like working or exercising. What differences do you see between the two lists?

It's time for a CHANGE

Lord, help me to have a pure and right heart when I...

Who Said THAT?

"It is not enough to take steps which may some day lead to a goal; each step must be itself a goal and a step likewise."

—Goethe

"Customer Service" in Children's Ministry

Think It Over

Have you ever had an irate parent give you a piece of her mind? How have you greeted a visitor, a guest, or a visiting relative of one of your children in the classroom? You are the face of your church to those parents. Your customer service skills are an important ingredient to reaching and keeping children and their parents.

the ART of TEACHING

Believe it or not, you do have customers! There are so many people you serve in your role that you may sometimes forget that you are providing a service and, therefore, have people you will please or offend! Parents have a choice of which church they'll attend. Children often persuade their parents not to come back because of a bad experience they've had. Pastors often hear from grateful parents about the awesome job the children's ministry has done for them. Here are some tips on creating a climate of superior customer service.

Be flexible! Your inflexibility means you are more interested in policies than people. Have you ever requested a government agency to consider the special circumstances of your request or situation? There is nothing more frustrating than an inflexible policy that does not make sense for a specific situation. Some policies and rules cannot have exceptions, and most policies are made for the good of the group rather than the individual. For example, parents should always sign in and sign out their children without exception. However, you can always look for ways to go above and beyond your customers' expectations. For example, if you are responsible for receiving children into your classroom, you could hand a bulletin or sermon notes to the parents as they sign in their children.

If you enter your classroom with the attitude that you are doing parents a favor, it's time to change your attitude. As a teacher, you have the God-given opportunity and responsibility to serve parents and children. You get to assist parents with helping their children understand the love of God. You also get to minister that same love to parents directly. You get to see the eternal fruit of your work here on earth and when you get to heaven. Serve parents and children faithfully and humbly, constantly remembering that it is a privilege to do so. ■

Customer Service

Serious Service

Nordstrom department store is notorious for its insistence on stellar customer service. With their employees, there's only one rule: "Use good judgment in all situations." Service is a core value at Nordstrom, and the customer is always right. Nordstrom apparently accepted a returned tire even though they don't sell tires!

SCRIPTURES *to Study*
✱ Commit it to MEMORY

"A gentle answer turns away wrath, but a harsh word stirs up anger."

—Proverbs 15:1

■ What helps you form a soft answer?

■ How have you been doing with parents? with children?

Take It Home

Customer service is usually judged more by our reaction to stress than our actions when things are going smoothly. Take the following test. You'll need a bouncy ball that bounces wildly. Your goal is to bounce the ball into the kitchen sink or into a can you've set onto a table or someplace high. Take about five shots with the ball, and answer the following questions. What was it like to try to get the ball into the can? How did you feel when it didn't get in? How is that like or unlike dealing with people or children in your ministry?

TIC... TOC... TIC...

It's time for a CHANGE

Lord, please take my heart and make it ready to serve you by...

Who Said THAT?

"Service is the rent that you pay for room on this earth."

—Shirley Chisholm

Dealing With Grief

Think It Over

When a child is hurt physically, you immediately try to stop the pain, heal the hurt, and help the child rejoin friends. When a child is more deeply pained because of tragedy, the response for healing is more difficult to ascertain. But your unique position in the lives of children creates a unique opportunity to share God's love with them. Who in your children's ministry is hurting?

We grieve but not as those who do not have hope...

the ART of TEACHING

One of the preschool workers had just taken his life. While this was a tragedy at many levels, the most immediate concern was helping children in the classroom. The Mothers of Preschoolers moms gathered for a special meeting to learn how to explain this event to their children. Everyone was nearly in tears when they heard the news, and the sobs were muffled with now-moist tissue.

Children experience grief in much different ways from adults. A child's response to grief is based in large part on his or her inexperience with death, the lack of an adult-rich memory of the loved one, and an innate innocence and wonder that comes with childhood. But the experiences they have with grief impact their later years and their ability to process grief in the future.

When you help children deal with grief, control your own response in a way that allows you, as an adult, to clearly connect with the response of the child. If you are not ready to do that, wait until you are. Speak in slow, deliberate, and concrete sentences: "Dave died yesterday, and we are going to miss him." Wait for a response, but don't go beyond what a child can and wants to hear. The child may just want to play right away and get everything back to normal. Using euphemisms such as "Grandma is sleeping" may cause confusion or undue fear—a child may fear going to sleep or think that Grandma may wake up.

Make sure parents are included in the process. Ask parents what they have shared with their children and what they would like you to share. Encourage parents to watch for unusual signs of fear or confusion. Children may not want to sleep or may be afraid more than usual. Both parents and teachers should allow children to adjust on their own and then gently guide them back into a routine.

Most important, make sure children know that you are there for them. Don't over-promise by saying things such as "I won't ever leave you." But don't overexpose them to the harsh realities of life. Help children see that you don't know all the answers but you trust that God knows and that God is good. This is a great time to take the opportunity to avoid "grieving as those who have no hope." You can grieve and cry and miss the person who is gone, offering hope for a good future. ∎

Grief is a deeply personal response to tragedy, pain, or some other awful reality. When cooking with an onion, there is an inevitable response when trying to cut that onion. Take an onion and cut it in half. Then score the onion in a crisscross pattern deep enough for the horizontal slice to create chopped onions. As you are doing this, answer the following questions. What is my initial response to cutting this onion? How is that like or unlike my own response to loss or pain? What could I do to avoid this particular response next time? What would I miss by doing this?

"Mommy...?"

A friend of mine had a young son with an aggressive form of cancer. The progress of the disease was so slow that it allowed for many nights of quiet conversations about God and life and death. The conversation one night between mother and son took on an almost surreal quality. They were discussing the funeral service that the little boy would want, the casket, and even the music. "Mommy?" the little boy quietly shifted in his seat and stared straight at his mother.

"What honey?"

"Will it hurt when I die?"

The thoughts of a child are often more precious than our good adult answers could ever claim.

It's time for a CHANGE

Open my heart to feel deeply what others feel, to show mercy and compassion by...

SCRIPTURES to Study
✱ Commit it to MEMORY

"Rejoice with those who rejoice; mourn with those who mourn."

—Romans 12:15

■ What does it look like to mourn when others are mourning?

■ What happens when we join others in rejoicing and mourning?

Who Said THAT?

"While grief is fresh, every attempt to divert only irritates. You must wait till grief be digested."

—Samuel Johnson

We Have Visitors!

Eanie, meanie, minie, moe...
Through which door shall I go?

Think It Over

Imagine that you just graduated from a small high school and are starting college at a big university. You were sick the first week of classes and arrive ten minutes after the start of your first morning class. You stand outside the classroom and look in. All the people are in pairs, talking about some very large words being projected on a screen. You notice that most of them have laptop computers with them. You do not own one. Just as you are about to walk away, the teacher catches your eye. What is the worst possible thing that could happen next? What is the best possible thing that could happen?

the ART of TEACHING

All of us have at one time or another been the new kid in a situation. We have all felt apprehensive, timid, and shy. New children are common to children's ministry classrooms. People move often today, and people are also accustomed to church shopping throughout the year. Guests and relatives of members are also a common sight. Sometimes a visitor will only be in your presence one time in his or her entire life, so it is imperative that you make that one visit in your classroom a memorable and positive experience.

The first thing a new child in a classroom will notice is the level of warmth and acceptance he or she feels. Does the teacher go out of his or her way to say hello? Does the teacher introduce the rest of the class? Does he or she take the time to get down at the child's level to talk? You don't know if the child has ever heard the name of Jesus in his or her life. It is your responsibility to be Jesus' representative for the class time. That may sound intimidating, but it's possible with God's help. You will be able to show love and kindness, and that is just what the child needs.

Once children feel welcomed in the classroom, they then need to know that they are physically and emotionally safe. Most children have a fear of the unknown. Teachers can help alleviate this fear by restating the rules of the classroom and expressing expectations of children. When a new child hears that mean language and pushing will never be tolerated, the child feels more comfortable in a situation.

Children are very concerned about fitting in. "What if I don't know what the teacher is talking about? What if the other kids have different clothes on from mine? What if they already have friends and don't want to talk with me? What if...what if...what if..." As teachers, we may be talking about the story of Noah, but the new child's mind is racing with "what ifs." We can help alleviate those fears by fostering a loving environment in the classroom. Gently including without putting the new child on the spot will ease the situation. Outside of the new child's hearing, assign one or two of your regulars to make the new child feel included. Welcoming a child into God's kingdom is such a glorious job. Always make sure your class can feel how glorious the opportunity can be. ■

Visiting a King!

John Adams was the first ambassador to be selected to represent the newly victorious United States of America before the King of England, George III. Their first meeting filled John Adams with a great deal of anxiety because he was to deliver a prepared brief speech in which he would present his credentials. John Adams was given a private audience and told exactly what to do. First, he was to deliver a brief speech, and it was to be as complimentary as possible. Second, upon arrival in the room where he would meet the king, Adams was instructed to make three bows or "reverences." The first he would make upon entering the king's bedchamber (which was not where the king slept). The second bow was to be made halfway across the room, and the final bow was to be made before "the presence."

SCRIPTURES to Study
Commit it to MEMORY

"Greet one another with a holy kiss."

—1 Corinthians 16:20b

■ What is the best way you would like to be greeted in a new situation?

■ What does this mean for greeting children in our classroom?

Take It Home

Sometime in the week, go into a new store that you have never been in before. If you normally don't like hardware stores, pick that one. If you normally would never enter a cooking store, try that one. As you enter, look around and see what you notice first. What products catch your eye? Where are the employees in the store? Do any of them make eye contact with you? Do they ask if you need help? Is it possible to be given too much attention? (If you answered "no," go immediately to a store with commissioned sales people and see how your answer can change.) What things in the store would make you want to come back again? What things would make you want to look for a different store in the future? How can you relate this to being new in a church?

God is trying to show me ways to welcome children into his kingdom. I can do this more effectively by...

"If a man be gracious and courteous to strangers, it shows he is a citizen of the world."

—Francis Bacon

Great Expectations

Think It Over

The good news is that you have one or two complete hours every week to help shape, encourage, and teach children. The bad news is that your time with each child is only 1/168th of his or her entire week and less than 1/100th of the hours a child spends awake. You have a lot to do in a very short amount of time. How can you make sure you are making a big impact with the time you have?

the ART of TEACHING

There are so many different strategies and approaches you can take in your classroom. There are so many models of ministry from which to choose. There are so many curricula from which to choose, so many activities you can lead, and so many different ways to teach the children in your class.

However you choose to teach, you must remember that your time with each child is precious. If a child comes to your class *every* week for an hour, you will spend 52 hours with that child in an entire year. You have 52 hours out of a child's 5,475 waking hours—less than 1 percent of a child's time. Yet the lessons you are delivering are the most important lessons a child will ever hear.

The primary unstated goal of many Sunday school teachers is to simply survive the hour in the classroom. Well-meaning teachers look for ways to stretch activities and fill time to keep children occupied while the "real" ministry takes place in the adult service. This mind-set is absolutely unacceptable when we consider how precious our time with children really is. We must be very intentional with the short amount of time we are given to teach and influence the children in our classes.

It's important to think through every activity and experience we provide for children. Look at every aspect of your class time and ask, "What are we accomplishing by doing this?" If you find that a routine or a method doesn't serve much purpose, eliminate it and replace it with something meaningful. This does not mean that you should throw out everything except activities that provide serious Bible content. Bible content is an essential aspect of Sunday school; however, children need to build relationships with other Christian kids and adults. Children also need to discover, explore, and have fun.

Rather than overreacting and shoving as much content as possible into a small amount of time, simply evaluate the benefit of what children are doing. Outline the goals you have in teaching, give weight to each goal, and then make sure the use of your class time reflects those goals. Then teach with purpose and passion—there's no time to lose! ■

Making the Most of It —

The typical field trip of most school-age children is a visit to the local zoo, the children's museum, or the library. In the past, these have been breaks from the routine of school but nothing more. Today, however, many museums are transforming the way they design their buildings to compete for children's attention.

The Children's Museum of Memphis, Tennessee, recently featured an exhibit called "Brain Teasers 2," a collection of puzzles that hone problem-solving skills by having children arrange geometric shapes to form new ones. They even had families team up to help solve many of the puzzles.

The Cleveland museum for kids has an exhibit that provides hands-on learning about weather and water systems. It includes a two-story climbing structure that demonstrates the water cycle.

The Indianapolis Children's Museum built an exhibition that was inspired by the children's book *Busytown* by Richard Scarry.

Take It Home

The next time you sit with your family, discuss your last vacation. Have each person relay the best and the worst experiences he or she had on vacation. Then ask yourself, "How was our vacation memory like or unlike what I want for my children this next Sunday?"

It's time for a CHANGE

Help me to use the class time you have given me with children to...

SCRIPTURES to Study
* Commit it to MEMORY

"Remember the wonders he has done, his miracles, and the judgments he pronounced."

—1 Chronicles 16:12

■ Why would God want you to remember the awesome miracles he has done?

■ What do you want your pupils to remember about lessons?

Who Said THAT?

"The Law of Primacy...states that the earlier an experience the more potent its effect since it influences how later experiences will be interpreted."

—J.A.C. Brown,
Techniques of Persuasion: From Propaganda to Brainwashing

Spiritual Assessment

Think It Over

Are the children in

your classroom closer

to God today than

when you started?

How do you know?

How can we tell if

children are growing

spiritually?

the ART of TEACHING

Woody Allen once said, "Eighty percent of success is showing up." When it comes to ministry, attendance may be only one of the concrete indicators we have for our ministry. We don't give out report cards, we don't take tests, and we never spring pop quizzes. Just what kind of school is this anyway?

Attendance and numbers do not necessarily indicate success. You can know if you've succeeded this week by asking some key questions of some key individuals.

Ask parents to pinpoint specific behavioral changes in their children's interactions with peers, siblings, and other adults. Ask parents if they have any evidence of how your ministry is affecting their children; however, parents may not be able to site specific examples even if God has done significant work through your teaching. Any change, no matter how small, can be a key indicator that you are having an effect. Such conversations with parents provide you with an excellent opportunity to discover areas for needed growth in your children and opportunities to reinforce the specific spiritual goals parents have for their children.

Asking the children about their spiritual growth can give you insight into a child's progress as well as provide excellent ministry opportunities. Asking open-ended questions such as "How you were able to show kindness to someone who was hurt this past week?" will tell you much more than the tired factual-recall questions such as "Now class, what did we talk about last week?"

Finally, work with your co-workers and leaders to determine how what you are doing is making a difference. Do the pictures children make and the questions children ask show a greater degree of understanding than they did at the beginning of the year? Are children's prayers connecting with the heart rather than relaying information? Are children finding comfort in God, understanding that Jesus loves them, and engaging in group or pair work?

It's important to remember not to take too much credit or too much blame regarding a child's spiritual development. Remember that you are God's vessel to bring his Word to children. The Holy Spirit gives your lessons their real power and impact. As you evaluate the growth of the children in your classroom, endeavor to provide the greatest opportunities for the Holy Spirit to do his work. ■

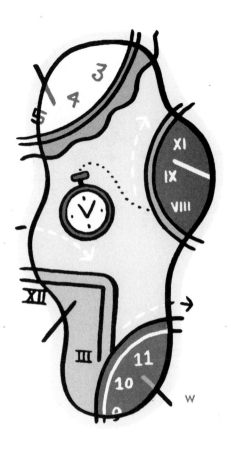

Some Things Take Time

Euclid told Ptolemy I, the king of Egypt, that mastering geometry would require long hours of study and memorization. When the pharaoh complained about the work, Euclid replied, "There is no royal road to geometry."

SCRIPTURES *to Study*
* Commit it to MEMORY

"I planted the seed, Apollos watered it, but God made it grow. So neither he who plants nor he who waters is anything, but only God, who makes things grow."

—1 Corinthians 3:6-7

■ What is God's role in spiritual development?

■ What grade do you think the Lord would give your teaching?

Take It Home

The true test of our faith is in how it is lived. Gather several twigs. Try snapping one. Pretty easy, isn't it? Now try snapping several together. What does this experiment say about what it takes to help children grow strong in their faith?

It's time for a CHANGE

Lord, help me never be satisfied with yesterday's success of...

Who Said THAT?

"Young man, the secret of my success is that at an early age I discovered I was not God."

—Oliver Wendell Holmes, Jr.

Multiply Your Ministry

Think It Over

Moses mentored Joshua and eventually transferred his ministry to his apprentice. Elisha carried on the ministry of Elijah. Jesus had eleven faithful disciples to preach the good news. Who are you mentoring and developing right now to minister to the next generation?

I just don't know what we are going to do without Mrs. Williams. She has been teaching the 3-year-old class for over 20 years!

the ART of TEACHING

Many businesses have shut down, broken apart, or simply fizzled out because the CEO and board failed to acknowledge the necessity of a succession plan. Other companies have chosen a new leader who is so clearly unprepared and inferior that he or she made the retiring CEO look stellar and indispensable in comparison. You may be able to minister to the children in your class for a long time, but you can't do it forever. And if your ministry is to grow, you must raise up new leaders who can care for the new children God will bring to your church.

Acknowledging that you even need to find a replacement creates a sense of vision for the future. Your church is in trouble if the future of children's ministry or the future of your classroom rests entirely on you. If God calls you somewhere else or to another ministry, your children's ministry should be able to move forward. Finding a replacement doesn't necessarily mean that you will move on from the children's ministry. In fact, training your replacement will free up your time and energy to take your classroom and your ministry to new levels.

Every thriving ministry should be looking to identify, train, and release new leaders. Your search should begin as you are developing competence as a teacher rather than when you are ready to retire or resign. Prospective teachers who spend time with you should increase in their own passion for children because of your influence. A replacement multiplies your ministry to reach more children for Jesus Christ. A church cannot grow by simply adding seekers and members. It must have trained leaders to help new members grow in faith.

Many ministries require their leaders to identify and train new leaders. As a teacher, you have an opportunity to touch the lives of many children. For each leader you identify, train, and release, your potential reach and influence doubles. There is nothing more satisfying in ministry than to help a person who didn't even know he or she could reach a child become a competent and enthusiastic teacher. ■

It's a good thing she asked me to help teach this past year. Otherwise, I would have never known what a wonderful ministry this was!

A Leader With Vision ——

When Margaret Thatcher's term as Prime Minister of Great Britain was ending, she said, "But there was one more duty I had to perform, and that was to ensure that John Major was my successor. I wanted—perhaps I needed—to believe that he was the man to secure and safeguard my legacy and to take our policies forward."

![Scriptures to Study] **SCRIPTURES** *to Study*
* Commit it to **MEMORY**

"Simon, Simon, Satan has asked to sift you as wheat. But I have prayed for you, Simon, that your faith may not fail. And when you have turned back, strengthen your brothers."

—Luke 22:31-32

■ What does the verse above tell you about people learning in spite of their limitations?

■ How should this verse encourage your own effort to "strengthen" your co-laborers?

Take It Home

The most logical replacements for our ministry positions are the gifted and qualified leaders in the church. You may be frustrated to find that the gifted leaders are already engaged in many ministries. Rather than looking for proven leaders, think about all of the potential leaders in your church. What a joy it is to develop leaders who previously didn't understand their place or value in God's kingdom. Make a list of all the people you know who are potential children's ministry leaders.

It's time for a CHANGE

Lord, open my eyes to see those whom you have already selected to carry on your love for your children by...

Who Said THAT?

"And the things you have heard me say in the presence of many witnesses entrust to reliable men who will also be qualified to teach others."

—Paul to Timothy (2 Timothy 2:2)

Attitude Is Everything!

What face should we put on Mrs. Johnson today?

Think It Over

There are not many choices in your role as a teacher. You may not choose your students; you may not even choose your classroom. You might not choose your curriculum, and you might not choose your co-workers. You don't always choose your leader, and you don't choose your classroom furniture. But you can choose your attitude.

the ART of TEACHING

Have you ever felt lethargic? really listless and unable to do anything? What do you do to get yourself going? How do you thaw out your frozen inertia? Have you ever felt so bubbly that you caffeinate everyone with whom you come into contact? Could your energy power a small village? Are you so exuberant that it is difficult to calm down?

No matter what your energy level is, your attitude is your choice! You power the train from which you teach, and your students are clearly affected by your attitude! If you love teaching, it shows. If you can't stand being in the classroom, children feel it. Your attitude affects everything to which you put your hands.

Your attitude affects your relationship with Christ. Is your love for the living Christ evident in your face? Like Moses, does your skin glow because you've spent time with your God? Is the fruit of your life bending the vine, or is it ready to be boxed up like raisins? God is readily available to support, help, and connect with his children. Is your attitude getting in the way of that connection?

Your attitude affects your relationships with your students. Educators have long noted the "Pygmalion Effect," which states that a student will behave up to the teacher's expectations. The same idea has been referred to as self-fulfilling prophecy. You will live up to your expectations, and your results will often match your dream of success or failure. Are you a teacher with high expectations for each student? Do you see the potential in each student God has given you?

Your attitude affects your role and success as a teacher. Teaching can be tough. Teachers are guaranteed hard work. But you can reflect joy during the highs and lows of teaching. You determine if you handle adversity as an opportunity to grow or an excuse to complain. Can you look at struggle as God's hand shaping you into a more effective teacher and disciple? Can you look for the good God is doing in the middle of the bad you're facing? Your answer to these questions will determine the outcome of the difficulties you are certain to face. ∎

A Shaping Attitude ———

My favorite teacher growing up was a new teacher in a school that was old and overdue for a remodel. Mrs. Ussery was remarkable for what she made us feel about ourselves as a group of students. She helped us all try to do things for ourselves, which was a contrast from our old teachers who would color a page and have us all try to imitate their art.

One day, my tooth was loose. Mrs. Ussery was a little skittish about pulling teeth, so she lassoed my tooth with a string and sent me in the hallway because she couldn't bear to watch. Left alone, I learned I could pull my own teeth! I felt so grown up.

We put on plays, read books that were classics *and* full of adventure, and even gave speeches that we had to prepare by ourselves. Never once did she scold or get angry. She let us discover things for ourselves! People rarely remember what you say, they rarely remember what you do, but I never forgot the way Mrs. Ussery made me feel!

Take It Home

Paul understood the difference between actions and attitudes in the familiar command to children in Ephesians 6. First he encourages us to obey our parents in the Lord, for this is right. He then reminds us to honor our father and mother. Honor is an attitude, while obedience is an action. How do your actions match your attitude?

It's time for a CHANGE

Change my heart and my attitude to reflect your own by...

SCRIPTURES *to Study*
* Commit it to MEMORY

"Your attitude should be the same as that of Christ Jesus: Who, being in very nature God, did not consider equality with God something to be grasped, but made himself nothing, taking the very nature of a servant, being made in human likeness."

—Philippians 2:5-7

■ What does a humble attitude look like for you?

■ How has your attitude been lately?

Who Said THAT?

"Enthusiasm signifies God in us."

—Madame de Staël,
De l'Allenmagne

Nice Serve!

What else can we help you with today?

Think It Over

Everyone knows that the teacher learns more about the subject that he or she is teaching than the students learn. Do you think the same could be said about people who serve? If so, how are you teaching the children in your class to serve others?

the ART of TEACHING

Does the thought of adding service activities and ideas to your curriculum overwhelm you? Maybe your curriculum already has too many activities. You know you have to fit in stories, crafts, snacks, songs, and games to be effective, and now you're supposed to come up with a service project. *Help!* You may feel like you are about to become a service project for the church to piece back together.

Take a deep breath, and ask the Holy Spirit to fill your lungs. Your service project doesn't necessarily have to be another item added to your to-do list for children. In fact, you can think of a service project as a temporary replacement to the part of your lesson you like least. For example, if your craft time is just one big mess, you can replace it with work on the service project for a little while.

Service projects do not have to be large-scale productions. You can take class time to make bird feeders, make presents for visitors, create a cookbook, write to pen pals or sponsored children, and clip grocery coupons for a local food bank. If you are able to take the service project beyond the classroom, the opportunities are limited only by your imagination. You could clear a vacant lot, paint a fence, decorate an area of your church, pick vegetables in a farmer's field to donate to people in need, or make a prayer chain.

Whatever you decide to do, work to allow children to see how their labor affects actual people. For example, if your class sponsors a child through an organization like World Vision, make sure children see the child's photograph, hear or read the child's letter, and are given an opportunity to write letters or contribute to the gifts the organization requests. If your class creates a food basket, ask the person you deliver it to if you can record his or her response on video so you can show it to the children.

Children want to make a difference. Service projects make people feel a part of life rather than feeling apart from life. They give children a feeling of empowerment. Service increases their self-esteem and love for mankind. It allows us to wash people's feet if only for a brief moment and see the beauty that Jesus saw in the act of servanthood.

Now go ahead; it's your serve! ■

A Lot of Work

According to the United States Department of Labor's Bureau of Labor Statistics, 59 million people did volunteer work in the United States from September 2001 to September 2002. Some interesting results were witnessed:

The volunteer rate was higher among women than men.

Thirty-five- to fifty-four-year-olds were more likely to donate their time: 33 percent.

Volunteer rates were lowest among persons age 65 years and over: 22.7 percent.

Teenagers had a higher rate (26.9 percent) than those in their early twenties (18.2 percent).

The main organization for which the majority of volunteers worked was either religious (33.9 percent) or educational (27.2 percent).

Most volunteers provide their services to one organization (69.1 percent).

Teaching or coaching is the most reported activity (24.4 percent) followed by campaigning or fund raising (22.9 percent).

Forty percent of volunteers became involved on their own initiative, and another 40 percent were asked to volunteer.

Take It Home

Play the childhood game of Ding-Dong Ditch. Think of something that you would like to secretly give a neighbor or a family member. It could be a food item, a trinket, a happy note, or a book. Now secretly put the item near the person's door, ring the doorbell, and run. Now comes the hard part. Tell no one...ever. Is it hard to keep a secret about acts of kindness? How can we teach children that they do not need credit for good things they do?

It's time for a CHANGE

I think I can become a better servant by...

SCRIPTURES to Study
* Commit it to MEMORY

"Now that I, your Lord and Teacher, have washed your feet, you also should wash one another's feet. I have set an example that you should do as I have done for you."

—John 13:14-15

■ What acts of servanthood have you done recently?

■ What does this tell us about our purpose here on earth?

Who Said THAT?

"And so, my fellow Americans: ask not what your country can do for you—ask what you can do for your country."

—John Fitzgerald Kennedy, conclusion of his Inaugural Address, January 20, 1961

10 Tips for Effective Meetings

*T*eacher Training on the Go is an important part of empowering your teachers, but it's not the only part. Teacher training meetings provide opportunities for your team to build relationship, find support, and deal with the unique problems of your ministry. When you hold your training meetings, you might want to keep the following things in mind.

■ First, feed the flock! You might not want to serve an entire dinner, but finger food should be in abundant supply. Subway sandwiches, pizzas, or salad bars go a long way to satisfying hungry appetites. Sharing food helps us bond together and relax and puts us in a better mood for learning.

■ Second, think about door prizes! LuAnne Oklobzija, Children's Pastor at Eagle Brook Church in White Bear Lake, Minnesota, gives out dinner gift certificates, Blockbuster video gift certificates, and even Home Depot gift certificates! You can tie your prizes directly to the service and work of your volunteers. You say you appreciate your volunteers and that they're important to the church. Here's a chance for your church to put its money where its mouth is.

■ Third, advertise your topic. Don't advertise your meeting! "Quarterly Teacher Training" just doesn't seem to excite the volunteers as much as "Handling Active Kids in a Lively Classroom" or "How to Talk so Kids Will Listen and Listen so Kids Will Talk." Also, let people know when the event will *end*, not just when it will start. This will help them plan around it, set up realistic expectations, and keep you on schedule.

■ Fourth, don't limit yourself to one topic! Have breakout sessions for age-appropriate team meetings. Noreen Richenbach, Children's Pastor at North Heights Lutheran Church in Arden Hills, invites publishers to send their representatives (for free) to do a mini-Sunday school convention! There is a time of worship just before several breakout sessions covering age-appropriate topics. Then she ends with lunch for everyone.

■ Fifth, child care is a must. Even if people do not use it, just offering it will eliminate that inevitable excuse not to attend. Remember, if you serve food, chances are your volunteers have not fed their children and will assume the food is for their kids as well. Have a separate area for pizza for kids, or just have food at the outset and let parents eat with their children. If you don't have volunteers who can help out with the kids, hire sitters from your church or from a local day care.

■ Sixth, plan for training well in advance by budgeting for it. Your training and development budget should be well planned to cover the amount of training you will do as well as the frequency of training. An unplanned expense has a much greater chance of being rejected by the budget committee. As you prepare your budget request, be prepared to explain how having trained teachers limits the liability of the church as well as produces effective ministry.

■ Seventh, work to specialize your training. There are some topics that will appeal to your midweek elementary volunteer as well as your once-a-month nursery volunteer. The fact is, not every training opportunity will meet everyone's needs. Have a separate training for your nursery volunteers that covers handling the "customer" in a pleasant manner. There is an appeal to getting everyone together for support and camaraderie. You can begin together and cover the global issues, then move into smaller groups for specialized training.

■ Eighth, let someone else help you. Sign up your volunteers to attend the local Sunday school convention, and go with them. For a list of conventions in your area, call your local Christian bookstore or the Church Ministries Convention Network. Attend one of the Children's Ministry Magazine "Live" events with your volunteer team. Take them "outlet" shopping on the way home, or debrief over coffee and cheesecake at your house. In other words, make a memory that will keep them going 'til the next training event.

■ Ninth, never give up! Try everything! Remember, even the largest churches only get 30 percent of their volunteers to attend any given training event. Have a Thursday night training event that ends before 8:30 (when kids need to get to bed). Hold the training during the Sunday morning time when your teachers would have been teaching. Hold the training during a midweek program when there is already something for their children. If one topic does not succeed, try another! Have your senior pastor show up unannounced and sit with the group to learn along with everyone else. Keep adjusting and improving even when it seems that what you already do works fine.

■ Tenth, don't call it *teacher* training. Not all your volunteers are teachers, and not all your training is for those with a title. Some other descriptions include "volunteer enrichment," "shepherd's training," or even "children's ministry meetings."

Theme Index

Each of the following E-couragement Blasts are included electronically in Rich Text Format (RTF) and PDF format on the enclosed CD-ROM. Feel free to edit them to match your ministry and the needs of your volunteers. They're sure to appreciate the e-couraging words!

Check Your Attitude

Thought for Today

As you're heading to the classroom this Sunday, how is your attitude? Have you had a long week? Has it been full of busyness and responsibilities? Are you tired? If you are, that's OK! God's Word tells us that his strength is made perfect in our weakness (2 Corinthians 12:9). You have everything you need through the Holy Spirit to be the teacher those students need. Lean into him today!

Quote for Today

Viktor Frankl, Auschwitz survivor and the author of *Man's Search for Meaning* writes,

"We who lived in concentration camps can remember the men who walked through the huts comforting others, giving away their last piece of bread. They may have been few in number, but they offer sufficient proof that everything can be taken from a man but one thing: the last of the human freedoms—to choose one's attitude in any given set of circumstances, to choose one's own way."

Scripture for Today

"But he said to me, 'My grace is sufficient for you, for my power is made perfect in weakness.' Therefore I will boast all the more gladly about my weaknesses, so that Christ's power may rest on me."

2 Corinthians 12:9

Check Your Focus

Thought for Today

Think of a camera lens. You want your photo not blurred, your object centered, your finger out of the way of the shutter. How do you accomplish that? First you have to stop. Be still. Maybe take a deep breath so the camera is steady. Be still this week, dear worker. Sit quietly before our Lord. Take a deep breath of his new mercies. Let your focus be on faith—your faith and the faith of your students.

Quote for Today

"*Grand Inquisitor.* The secret of man's being is not only to live but to have something to live for."

—Fyodor Dostoyevsky
(*The Brothers Karamazov*)

Scripture for Today

"Set your mind on things above, not on earthly things."

Colossians 3:2

Published in *Teacher Training on the Go* by Group Publishing, Inc., P.O. Box 481, Loveland, CO 80539. www.grouppublishing.com

Check Your Preparation

Thought for Today

You're having a dinner party Friday night. Your guests will arrive at 6:00 p.m. When do you begin thinking about your evening? What will your guests be eating? What will the centerpiece look like? How do you want your guests to feel when they step through the door? How do you want them to feel when they gather their coats to leave?

You have sacrificed so much time, energy, emotion, and creativity to make your guests feel important. They only see the results, not the pain of preparation!

King David says in I Chronicles 21:24, "I insist on paying the full price. I will not take for the Lord what is yours, or sacrifice a burnt offering that costs me nothing." As you prepare to meet your class this week, honor them with your preparation. Think what God will say when he sees your sacrifice as you do your work heartily for the Lord!

Quote for Today

"Prepare your hearts for Death's cold hand! prepare

Your souls for flight, your bodies for the earth;

Prepare your arms for glorious victory;

Prepare your eyes to meet a holy God!

Prepare, prepare!"

—William Blake
(*A War Song to Englishmen*)

Scripture for Today

"See, I am sending an angel ahead of you to guard you along the way and to bring you to the place I have prepared."

Exodus 23:20

Check Your Commitment

Thought for Today

Do you know how to tell if someone is married? The most obvious sign is a ring on the ring finger of the left hand. There are much more significant signs of marriage. Affection, verbal promises, public confirmation, consistency over time, and children are important outward signs that demonstrate the commitment of marriage.

What are the signs of commitment in teaching? The most obvious is showing up on Sunday mornings, engaged and ready to teach. Other signs of your commitment include time on the job, showing up early, dedication, energy, preparation, and intensity. Second Chronicles 16:9 says that the "eyes of the Lord range throughout the earth to strengthen those whose hearts are fully committed to him." Let your prayer today be Psalm 71:18: "Even when I am old and gray, do not forsake me, O God, till I declare your power to the next generation, your might to all who are to come."

Be strengthened today by God for whom and through whom you teach!

Quote for Today

"Without passion man is a mere latent force and possibility, like the flint which awaits the shock of the iron before it can give forth its spark."

—Henri Amiel

Scripture for Today

"For the eyes of the Lord range throughout the earth to strengthen those whose hearts are fully committed to him."

2 Chronicles 16:9a

Check How Interesting You Are

Thought for Today

Have you ever tasted salt-free butter? What about sodium-free crackers? It's amazing to think that something as common as salt is all that changes a bland snack into a tasty treat.

You don't have to be a stand-up comedian to have a little spice and creativity in your teaching. We have been commanded to be salt and light, and God is fully aware of our deficiencies. His resources are limitless and available to all who will ask. He is standing ready to be the resource you need to take his Word to change the lives for which he died.

How can you add salt and light to this week's lesson?

Quote for Today

"That Man divine whom Wisdom calls her own,

Great without Title, without Fortune bless'd,

Rich ev'n when plunder'd, honor'd while oppress'd,

Lov'd without youth, and follow'd without power

At home tho' exil'd, free, tho' in the Tower."

—Alexander Pope
(*Imitations of Horace*)

Scripture for Today

"With this in mind, we constantly pray for you, that our God may count you worthy of his calling, and that by his power he may fulfill every good purpose of yours and every act prompted by your faith."

2 Thessalonians 1:11

Check Your Balance

Thought for Today

Do you get nervous about what funds you have available whenever you use your credit card? When you see the word *Approved* appear at the cash register, do you sigh with relief or simply ignore the announcement because you were already aware of the balance?

Knowing your balance is important when you go shopping in order to have a stress-free experience and to avoid serious bank charges. If your balance starts to get depleted, it is important to either add more money or stop spending.

This week, you have a balance that you need to check! It is your emotional and spiritual bank account from which you teach and give to others. You cannot impart what you do not possess!

If you can do all things through Christ who strengthens you, then it stands to reason that his strength is what you need!

Quote for Today

"There are two kinds of fool. One says, 'This is old, and therefore good.' And one says, 'This is new, and therefore better.'"

—John Brunner

Scripture for Today

"Who has measured the waters in the hollow of his hand, or with the breadth of his hand marked off the heavens? Who has held the dust of the earth in a basket, or weighed the mountains on the scales and the hills in a balance?"

Isaiah 40:12

Check Your Patience

Thought for Today

"I am not a patient person!" Have you ever heard anyone say that? Have you ever felt that way yourself? We all have at one time or another felt impatient. Maybe it happened on the freeway when the car beside you cut you off. Maybe it happened as you prepared dinner and your daughter demanded attention at that moment.

You cannot choose the fruit of the Spirit like fruits you pick and choose at a buffet. The fruit of the Spirit is all or nothing. If the Holy Spirit is in you, love, joy, peace, *patience*, kindness, goodness, faithfulness, gentleness, and self-control will all be evident in your actions and attitudes. We find out what is inside us by what comes out when we are squeezed. Check the fullness and growth of your patience by honestly evaluating how you react when things are difficult. Are you a patient person? Ask God, "who gives generously to all without finding fault" (James 1:5), to fill you up with the fruit of patience.

Quote for Today

"God, give us grace to accept with serenity the things which cannot be changed, courage to change the things which should be changed, and the wisdom to distinguish the one from the other."

—Reinhold Niebuhr

Scripture for Today

"Through patience a ruler can be persuaded, and a gentle tongue can break a bone."

Proverbs 25:15

Check Your Thoughts

Thought for Today

The battle for our hearts and our devotion begins in our thought life. If Satan can convince you of a certain thing in your mind, your actions will surely follow. If negative thoughts are allowed to linger, depression, anger, and discouragement will result. On the contrary, if we are obedient to the challenge of taking every thought captive to the obedience of Christ (2 Corinthians 10:5), we stop the Enemy dead in his tracks.

You are in charge of your thoughts! Your thoughts, in turn, are critical to how you act and feel. When your head hits the pillow tonight, it's just you and God. A clear conscience is a result of firm convictions and consistent actions.

Quote for Today

"A good Conscience is a continual Christmas."

—Benjamin Franklin
(*Poor Richard's Almanack*)

Scripture for Today

"We demolish arguments and every pretension that sets itself up against the knowledge of God, and we take captive every thought to make it obedient to Christ."

2 Corinthians 10:5

Check Your Blessings

Thought for Today

The Israelites were blessed by God but chose many times not to be a blessing to others or to God. Since every good and perfect thing comes from God, look around you and be overwhelmed by his good gifts.

When we take our eyes off his blessings, we begin to forget, tend to despair, and often feel like quitting. Isaiah 51:1 should be on your lips all week: "Listen to me, you who pursue righteousness and who seek the Lord: Look to the rock from which you were cut and to the quarry from which you were hewn." Remember your past in order to acknowledge God's hand in your future! Even if you've only been teaching for two weeks, you have the potential to improve, to be filled with God's blessing, and to grow. As you see God's blessing, ask how you can give it away! Remember, you can never out-give God, and he is ready to refill you and reuse you!

Quote for Today

"I possess tremendous power to make life miserable or joyous. I can be a tool of torture or an instrument of inspiration. I can humiliate or humor, hurt or heal. In all situations, it is my response that decides whether a crisis is escalated or de-escalated, and a person is humanized or de-humanized. If we take people only as they are, we make them worse; if we treat them as though they were what they ought to be, we steer them in the right direction."

—Goethe

Scripture for Today

"I will bless them and the places surrounding my hill. I will send down showers in season; there will be showers of blessing."

Ezekiel 34:26

Check Your Example

Thought for Today

The cliché "Actions speak louder than words" is over-spoken but often under-lived. First Timothy 4:12 says that we are not to allow anyone to look down on our young life or young faith but we are to "set an example for the believers in speech, in life, in love, in faith and in purity." What does your example say to the children in your classroom? Can they follow your example to find passion, joy, peace, and life in Christ?

Thank you for being a model Christian on the runway of children's ministry!

Quote for Today

"Example, the surest method of instruction."

—Pliny the Younger

Scripture for Today

"Now that I, your Lord and Teacher, have washed your feet, you also should wash one another's feet. I have set you an example that you should do as I have done for you. I tell you the truth, no servant is greater than his master, nor is a messenger greater than the one who sent him."

John 13:14-16

Check Your Resources

Thought for Today

It takes money to make money. If you want to start a new business, start a savings account, or make an investment, you need resources. A 401K or a college-savings plan most often provides a worthwhile dividend over the long haul of ten, twenty, or even forty years.

Ministry takes resources too. The investment you make in a child's life produces a dividend that lasts for eternity. You may not see the payoff of your work until your life is over, but this investment plan is more certain than your retirement plan or the most secure savings account.

While curriculum, meeting spaces, and supplies are important resources in children's ministry, you are our most valuable resource. The investment of opening up your life and heart to the children in your classroom has some risks, but the payoff is more than you can ever imagine.

Thank you for making an investment in this church, our children, and eternity!

Quote for Today

"Dare to look up to God and say, 'Make use of me for the future as Thou wilt...I refuse nothing which seems good to Thee. Lead me wither Thou wilt.'"

—Epictetus

Scripture for Today

"But the Counselor, the Holy Spirit, whom the Father will send in my name, will teach you all things and will remind you of everything I have said to you."

John 14:26

Published in *Teacher Training on the Go* by Group Publishing, Inc., P.O. Box 481, Loveland, CO 80539. www.grouppublishing.com

Check Your Expectations

Thought for Today

Love always protects, believes all things, endures all things, hopes all things. Love never fails. Did the lesson you so carefully prepared seem to fall on deaf ears? Did your students seem totally unaffected by your object lesson? Did the craft you planned flop? Have you ever gone home disappointed in your students or in yourself?

It's time to check your expectations. We want the children to have fun, and we want the lesson to have impact. But don't forget that God may have a different plan for your lesson. Maybe you were concentrating on an awesome object lesson when God was more concerned with a child who needed to talk about what was going on at home. Maybe you felt that no one really got the point of your lesson when God used the lesson to launch a child down the road to full-time ministry. You don't know what God is doing. You do the outside work; God does the inside work. Don't judge your lessons solely on what you see on the outside. God is love, and he never fails.

Quote for Today

" 'No eye has seen, no ear has heard, no mind has conceived what God has prepared for those who love him'—but God has revealed it to us by his Spirit."

—Paul (I Corinthians 2:9-10a)

Scripture for Today

" 'For I know the plans I have for you,' declares the Lord, 'plans to prosper you and not to harm you, plans to give you hope and a future.'"

Jeremiah 29:II

The Perfect Tools
for Relational Ministry!

Heartfelt Thanks for Helping Kids Love Jesus

Looking for a special way to express genuine appreciation to Sunday school teachers? Give 'em *Heartfelt Thanks!* This vibrant devotional is packed with heartwarming stories by seasoned teachers that reinforce the remarkable difference that can be made in the lives of students—even when no one seems to notice! Each inspirational account concludes with a personal prayer or devotional activity that injects a fresh perspective and rekindles a passion for fostering spiritual growth in children. It's the perfect gift!

ISBN 0-7644-2638-9

Heartfelt Thanks for Sunday School Teachers

How do you truly thank Sunday school teachers in a way that shows deep appreciation, encouragement and inspiration? Give them *Heartfelt Thanks!* Packed with vibrant full-color art, *Heartfelt Thanks for Sunday School Teachers* includes space for journaling and responding to ministry questions. This portable keepsake is a memorable and inspirational gift—have extras on hand to give away when someone needs encouragement.

Here's why this perfect gift builds team members:
+ Inspiration—Sunday school teachers share real-life stories
+ Scripture—Verses encourage
+ Reflection—Journal space for devotional thoughts & responses
Great for individual worship and devotional activities!

ISBN 0-7644-2433-5

Children's Ministry Leadership: The You-Can-Do-It Guide

Jim Wideman

You can be a next-level leader! Expert Jim Wideman empowers readers to be dynamic, effective and efficient ministry leaders. This guide gives you the best of the best from Jim's favorite workshops and keynote addresses he's presented. And this isn't just theory—it's practical advice brought to you from someone who has served in hundreds of children's ministry settings, both behind the scenes and on stage.

ISBN 0-7644-2527-7

Children's Ministry That Works! (Revised and Updated)

Expert help for your children's ministry, at your fingertips!

Get the best, proven-effective ideas and strategies for key areas of children's ministry from 27 top children's ministers: Craig Jutila, Jim Wideman, Christine Yount, Pat Verbal and others! 15 brand-new chapters. Great for new or veteran children's ministers and workers!

ISBN 0-7644-2407-6

Awesome Volunteers

Christine Yount

The editor of Children's Ministry Magazine created this how-to book for recruiting, training and keeping volunteers fired up. Includes extensive interviews, practical insights and useful principles.

ISBN 0-7644-2056-9

EVALUATION FOR

Teacher Training on the Go

Please help Group Publishing, Inc., continue to provide innovative and useful resources for ministry. Please take a moment to fill out this evaluation and mail or fax it to us. Thanks!

Group Publishing, Inc.
Attention: Product Development
P.O. Box 481
Loveland, CO 80539
Fax: (970) 292-4370

• • •

1. As a whole, this book has been (circle one)
   not very helpful   very helpful
   1   2   3   4   5   6   7   8   9   10

2. The best things about this book:

3. Ways this book could be improved:

4. Things I will change because of this book:

5. Other books I'd like to see Group publish in the future:

6. Would you be interested in field-testing future Group products and giving us your feedback? If so, please fill in the information below:

Name _____

Church Name _____

Denomination _____ Church Size_____

Church Address _____

City_____ State _____ ZIP _____

Church Phone _____

E-mail _____